Old York

Paul Chrystal

Monk Bar Portcullis in the early 60s.

Stenlake Publishing Ltd.

Text © Paul Chrystal, 2019.
First published in the United Kingdom, 2019,
by Stenlake Publishing Ltd.,
54-58 Mill Square,
Catrine, Ayrshire,
KA5 6RD

Telephone: 01290 551122
www.stenlake.co.uk

Printed by
Blissetts, Unit 1, Shield Drive,
West Cross Industrial Park, Brentford, TW8 9EX

ISBN 9781840338508

Acknowledgements

Thanks to Jenny Orwin at Bootham School, Susannah Harrison at the University of York and to Steve Lewis at The York Press for allowing me to plunder their archives, yet again; Tassadar@midlandsheritageforum for the fascinating photograph of Terry's clock; and to John Roden for permission to use the Minster football photograph originally published in his *The Minster School, York: A Centenary History 1903-2004*. Special thanks go to Ian Drake of Yorkshire Architectural and York Archaeological Society for permission to use photographs from the magnificent Evelyn Collection. The Evelyn Collection is accessible through YAYAS, www.yayas.free-online.co.uk

Further Reading

Rotherham, I.D., *Lost York in Colour*, Stroud, 2006.
An excellent and accessible history of York, told largely through scores of vivid and previously obscure images.

Sotheran, Catherine, *York Minster in Close Up – The Exterior*, York, 2019.
550 Photos and descriptions of the amazing carvings to be seen on the outside of the Minster – in close up. Contact: walkcr.yorkie@gmail.com

Sotheran, Catherine, *York in Close Up*, York, 2017.
A wonderful, innovative book detailing all the things about York we've all probably missed – from heraldry to weather vanes, from rainwater hoppers to tiled doorways. You don't know York until you've read this book.

Stanhope, P.J., *Quaint and Historic York Remembered*, York, 2016.
Celebrates the life and works of York Victorian artist and architect Edwin Ridsdale Tate. Fascinating, detailed and much-needed contribution to the literature on York's history and Victorian art and architecture. Beautifully illustrated.

Introduction

Once it's gone, it's gone. That's as good a summary of William Etty's profound words of warning to the 'planners' of York as any: 'Beware how you destroy your antiquities, guard them with religious care! They are what give you a decided character and superiority over other provincial cities. You have lost much, take care of what remains'. Etty (1787-1849), along with others including Dr W.A. Evelyn (1860-1935) and JB Morrell (1873-1963), fought long and hard to save many of York's treasures from destruction, and we have much to thank them for. Many of their victories can still be seen in the York of today, and the city is much the richer for it. Sadly, much, as Etty laments, was also lost but it would have been so much worse were it not for the diligence and passion of men such as these.

Writing in 1125 William of Malmesbury, the so-called father of British history, shows how little has really changed with regard to England's north-south divide: 'Next in rank after Canterbury is York...almost everything about the language of the North, and particularly of the people of York, is so crude and discordant that we southerners cannot understand it. This is because they are near to barbarian peoples [the Scots] and far from the English kings'. But, 600 years later, a generous Daniel Defoe was having none of it: 'There is abundance of good company here, and abundance of good families live here, for the sake of the good company and cheap living; a man converses here with all the world as effectually as at London.' Daniel Defoe, 'A Tour Thro' The Whole Island Of Great Britain', 1724. Perhaps the truth lies with a man who really knows: 'York is, of course, the guide-book man's paradise, and not without good reason, for if you want the past, here it is, weighing tons. J.B. Priestley, *English Journey*, 1933.

York is the only city where gates are streets and also bars are gates. Eboracum was occupied by the Romans from AD71 until AD410 when they left Britannia for good. Quintus Petilius Cerialis led the IXth Hispana Legion north to subdue the Brigantes and established a garrison here. Strategically York was of great significance, being of considerable military importance and a major communications centre. The Colonia covered 60 acres and the walls were 20 feet high and four feet thick in parts. The Praetorium is under the Minster, there is an amphitheatre and temple under Micklegate and a *forum basilica*, baths on the banks of the Ouse, a sewerage system in Bishophill, a VIth Victrix Legion column opposite the Minster and a statue of Constantine nearby to celebrate his being proclaimed Emperor here in AD306 on the death of his father, the Emperor Constantius Chlorus, and his conversion to Christianity, probably in 312. Septimius Severus, Rome's first black emperor, lived in York between 208 and 211; his sons, Caracalla and Geta, were declared co-Emperors in 198 and 209. Severus died in York in 211 and received a spectacular funeral in the city, but not before he had declared York to be the capital of Britannia Inferior. Hadrian visited too.

Constantine the Great was the only Roman Emperor to be proclaimed *Augustus* while in Britain; he converted to Christianity in a ceremony outside the Minster in 312 after seeing a vision of the cross when consulting his Roman gods before The Battle of the Milvian Bridge. York, thereby, became an early, vital centre of Christianity. We have Constantine to thank for Christmas, for it was he who organised the first festivities celebrating Christ's birth. A marble head of Constantine was found during an excavation in Stonegate.

Eoforwic is the Saxon name for York. Anglo Saxon York was the capital of Deira and then of Deira and Bernicia, later called Northumbria. In the early 7th century York was an increasingly important city: Paulinus of York (St. Paulinus) established a wooden church here, the forerunner of York Minster, in AD627; King Edwin of Northumbria was baptised in the same year. Eoforwic, means 'wild-boar town' in Old English; the later Jorvik means horse bay. It is possible that Eoforwice is a later name for Cair Ebrauc, one of the cities mentioned in the *Historia Brittonum* of about 830, founded in legend by Ebrauk.

Jorvik is the Viking name for York. The Viking army attacked the city on November 1st 866 under the command of Halfdan and Ivar the Boneless. York soon became the capital of the Viking kingdom in the north. In 954 the last Viking king, Eric Bloodaxe was expelled. Legend has it that Ivar was fair, big, strong, and one of the wisest men who has ever lived. The origin of the nickname is troublesome: some say that the bonelessness suggests that he suffered from erectile dysfunction, others a form of osteogenesis imperfecta or brittle bone disease, others still believe he earned it from his chubby face. Ivar was the son of Ragnar Lothbrok. In 865 Ivar, with his brother Halfdan Ragnarsson (Halfdene), led the Great Heathen Army and took East Anglia; the following year on November 1st they captured York. The date was no coincidence, it being All Saints Day when much of the population would have been preoccupied in the old cathedral. Ivar was also a famous berserker – Norse warriors who in Old Norse literature are reported to have fought in a frenzied, trance-like fury (from which our word *berserk* is derived). Berserkers worked themselves into a rage before battle, possibly helped by drugged foods.

Domesday York's entry tells us about the 1,418 houses in 1086 with such detail as 'Odo the Crossbowman has three dwellings, of Forne and Orne... Landric the carpenter has ten and half dwellings which the sheriff assigned to him'. King John, brother of Richard the Lionheart, awarded York its charter in 1212, 806 years ago, and signed the *Magna Carta* in 1215 with Walter de Grey, Archbishop of York.

York, because of its cloth trade and the ancillary industries associated with it in the 14th century, was described as 'the foremost industrial town in the North of England.' In 1384 there were 800 weavers in the city. This was short-lived though, and the trade in cloth declined to such a degree that a visitor to the city in the 17th century, Thomas Fuller, remarked: 'the foreign trade is like their river...low and flat.'

Celia Fiennes, that intrepid lady traveller who journeyed the length and breadth of the country, often with only one or two maids in attendance, visited York in 1697. This is how she described the River 'Ouise' and the mean streets of York in her journal *Great Journey to Newcastle and to Cornwall*: 'it bears Great Barges, it Looks muddy, its full of good ffish. We Eate very good Cod fish and Salmon and that at a pretty Cheape rate, tho' we were not in the best jnn for the Angel is the best in Cunny Streete. The houses are very Low and as indifferent as in any Country town and the Narrowness of ye Streetes makes it appear very mean'.

Daniel Defoe, in *A Tour Through the Whole Island of Great Britain* at first disagrees, describing 'considerable trade' with France, Norway and Portugal, and then, in contradiction, asserts that: 'here is no trade...except such as depends upon the confluence of the gentry.' This commercial lethargy was due to some extent both to the high price of coal which had to be shipped from the coalfields of the West Riding, and to the restrictive, exclusive attitude of the local Merchant Adventurers and their insistence that all traders had to be Freemen of the City up until 1827. Francis Drake records in his *Eboracum: or the History and Antiquities of the City of York*, that York in the 18th century had precious little industry and the only real commercial activity was butter exports, corn and wine trading.

Butchers were famously focused in Shambles. Less well-known traders had their own pitches: Ousegate and Castlegate were the haunt of lorimers (makers of bits and bridles) and spurriers; cutlers were to be found near St. Michael-le-Belfry; pinners at St. Crux; girdlers at Girdlergate (Church Street), Tanners near North Street (hence Tanner's Moat and Tanner Row); fishmongers on the Foss and Ouse Bridges; parchment and leather workers and prostitutes at Harlot Hill (St. Maurice's Road today), harlots fittingly also in Grope (Grape) Lane.

In the 19th and 20th centuries, the railway and confectionery industries were soon to change the industrial and commercial landscape beyond all recognition.

There is an inextricable association between English chocolate manufacturing with the Society of Friends, or Quakerism. Fry, Cadbury, Rowntree and Thorne of Leeds were all Quakers. Why was it that the chocolate industry at the end of the 19th century and in the early years of the 20th prospered largely under Quaker ownership? It is all the more remarkable, though, when we remember that in 1851 Quakers accounted for less than 0.1% of the 21 million population of England.

Friends were excluded from the only teaching universities in England at the time, Oxford and Cambridge, because of their non-conformism and the universities' association with Anglicanism; they were debarred from Parliament and the guilds; they were restricted in what they could and could not do as lawyers because they refused to take oaths; the arts were considered frivolous and they were disqualified from the armed services because they were usually pacifists. One of the few alternatives left to well-to-do young Quakers was to pursue a life in industry or business, and this is what many did. In doing so they often brought with them a tradition of high quality management and fair trading practices, rigorous scientific research and innovative technical development as well as a preoccupation with quality and a breathtakingly detailed attention to commercial administration. So Quakers entered business and industry: one of the emerging industries at the time was cocoa and chocolate – this was partly a result of increased affordability amongst the working classes who had more disposable income, lower taxes on imports which reduced prices in the shops, and improvements in quality, a better taste and less adulteration. What had been a luxury for the few was fast becoming an affordable indulgence for many. Moreover, cocoa and chocolate dovetailed perfectly with Quaker views on temperance; they were healthy beverages too, because their production and consumption entailed boiling what was often unclean water. One of the legacies of the frequent meetings routinely held by Quakers to spread the word was the building up of a strong network of dependable friends and contacts; this in turn, along with intermarriage amongst Quaker families, led to a tradition of mutual assistance and an ethical, enlightened attitude in business and industry, and to strong industrial partnerships, underpinned by unfaltering service and philanthropy to the community at large. All of this manifested itself in York through Rowntree's; as such Quakerism has had an immeasurable effect on the city in every way – commercially, socially, educationally and physically – for over a century.

Everyone knows Terry's and Rowntree's and Cravens, the confectioners. There were, however, at least two other chocolate makers in the city: York Confectionery Company founded in 1867 in Fossgate and Lazenby & Son (York) Ltd.

As the discussions over city centre and out of town retailing rumble on through the 21st century, it is interesting to quote from a letter published way back in August 1790 in the *York Chronicle*: 'If the inhabitants of this city would rouse themselves to some spirited exertions and the Corporation open the gates to all tradesman and manufacturers inclinable to settle amongst us, York might again lift up its head and recover its ancient consequence as a principal place of commerce.'

It seems that there is nothing new in the world: short-sighted and short-term councils and xenophobia were all the rage over 200 years ago too.

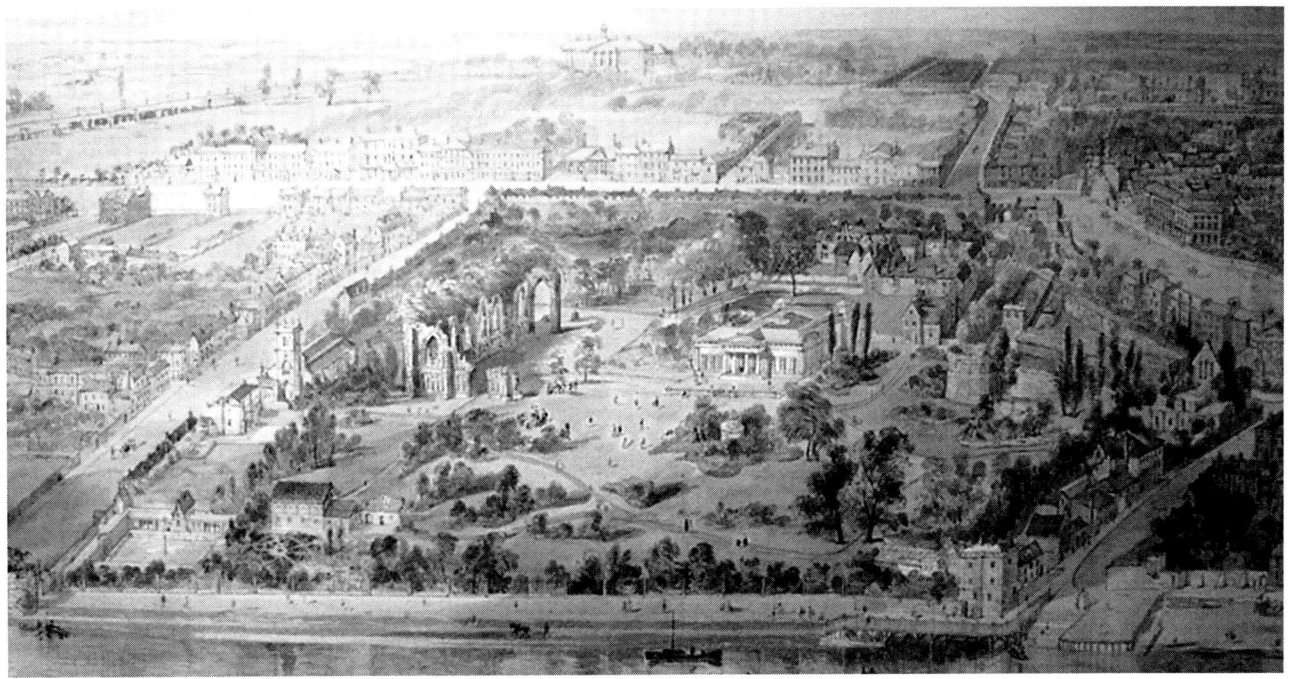

St. Mary's Abbey. One of the richest abbeys in the country, the Benedictines completed it in 1088. The surrounding walls (originally ¾ mile long) were built after townsfolk's attacks on the abbey when one of the clerics, Simon de Warwick, imposed taxes on the market along Bootham, outside the city walls. In 1132 Richard, the prior, and thirteen monks demanded a return to a traditionally simpler life which also involved giving away much of the abbey's money. After a near riot the rebels left York to found the much stricter Cistercian Fountains Abbey. Their departure had no impact on St. Mary's decadence which was celebrated in the *Ballads of Robin Hood*, one of whose enemies is a 'ryche abbot here besyde Of Seynt Mari Abbey'. The life-size stone saints and prophets painted in gold and other colours which adorned the west front of St. Mary's Abbey church are now in the Yorkshire Museum. They included Moses adorned with horns, typical of the mediaeval period due to a mistranslation of the Hebrew Bible into the Latin Vulgate Bible. The Hebrew word taken from *Exodus* can mean either a 'horn' or an 'irradiation' and in this case should be the latter; the most famous horned Moses is Michelangelo's statue in the Church of San Pietro in Vincoli, Rome.

A fitting place to start – with hope. Here are the massed ranks of delegates at the 9th British Esperanto Congress outside the Minster in 1916. Esperanto ('one who hopes') is the most widely spoken made-up language in the world; its name comes from Doktoro Esperanto the pseudonym under which physician and linguist L. L. Zamenhof published the first book detailing Esperanto, the *Unua Libro*, in 1887. Zamenhof's aim was 'to create an easy-to-learn, politically neutral language that would transcend nationality and foster peace and international understanding between people with different languages'. Up to 2 million people worldwide actively speak Esperanto, including 1,000 native speakers who learned Esperanto from birth.

Part of Newgate Market (or Shambles Market as it is known today) soon after the move from Parliament Steet in 1964. Parts of Jubbergate, Little Shambles and Silver Street were removed to make way. The site was fully revamped and reopened in March 2015 following a £1.6 million refurbishment.

Arriving for Work at Terry's of York in the 1950s. Terry's moved to their purpose-built Baroque Revival building in 1930 from the Clementhorpe site which they had occupied since 1862. By 1840 Terry's products including candied eringo, coltfoot rock, gum balls and lozenges made from squill, camphor and horehound were being delivered to 75 towns all over England. Apart from boiled sweets they also made marmalade, marzipan, mushroom ketchup and calves' jelly. Conversation lozenges, precursors of Love Hearts (with such slogans as 'Can you polka?', 'I want a wife', 'Do you love me?' and 'How do you flirt?'), were particularly popular. Chocolate production began around 1867 with thirteen chocolate products adding to the other 380 or so confectionery and parfait lines. Before the Second World War 'Theatre Chocolates' were available with rustle-proof wrappers. The famous Chocolate Orange (which started life as a Chocolate Apple) was born in 1932 and subsequently one in ten Christmas stockings reputedly contained a Terry's Chocolate Orange. In the 1990s seven million boxes of All Gold were sold in a year.

Civic Week, June 1928, St. Leonard's Place. A programme of events lasting a week, designed to showcase York as a place to visit. This is early evidence of the importance of tourism to York.

Window shopping in North Street in the 1920s.

This is what happened in York when the Prince of Wales (the future Edward VIII) came to town in 1923. Police and army reinforced by Girl Guides? This was at the time he was having an affair with socialite Freda Dudley Ward.

Bootham leavers 1873. William Tuke (1732-1822) first raised the idea in 1818 of setting up a boys' school in York for the sons of Quakers 'and any children of the opulent who will submit themselves to the general system of diet and discipline'. In 1822 premises on Lawrence Street were leased from the Retreat, and the school opened in early 1823 as the York Friends Boys' School, or 'The Appendage'. By 1829 it was known as Yorkshire Quarterly Meeting Boys' School – its official name until 1889 – even after it had moved to 20 (now 51) Bootham in 1846. It was the school's proximity to the River Foss that triggered the move to more salubrious premises; one master even carried a pistol to shoot the rats; cholera was also a problem. In the late 19th century many of the Rowntree family boys were educated at Bootham; one of them, Arthur Rowntree (or Chocolate Jumbo to give him his nickname), was Headmaster (1899-1927). The school had a tradition of taking disadvantaged boys from the Lawrence Street area on a Lads' Camp, usually at Robin Hood's Bay, and this endured well into the 20th century. Arthur Rowntree said: 'We are proud to be in the tradition of promoting friendship between all classes'. A number of staff and scholars were influential in the political and social reforms of their times, not least Seebohm Rowntree (Bootham 1882-87).

Bootham Natural History Society started in 1834 by John Ford, superintendent or head from 1829 to 1865. Its full name was The Natural History, Literary and Polytechnic Society and as such was the umbrella organisation for many other clubs. The school was moved to Roman Catholic Ampleforth during the Second World War; Donald Gray, the head at the time, is reputed to have addressed the combined school as 'Friends, Romans and Countrymen'. Bootham was not the only boys' Quaker School in York: in 1827 the Hope Street British School was established and attended by many children of Friends; it was slightly unusual because, in addition to the usual curriculum, it taught the working of the Electric Telegraph with the Electric Telegraph Company supplying the instruments and the school reciprocating by supplying the company with clerks. In 1899 almost the entire of Bootham school was destroyed by fire: a keen pupil was boiling snail shells in the natural history room when he was summoned by the bell for reading, and the snails were left boiling all night… on being informed by the fire brigade that his school was a smouldering shell the headmaster fell on his sword and promptly resigned. The accidental arsonist later became a farmer and blew himself up while uprooting a tree.

Flooding, March 1947. As surely as winter follows autumn so York will flood. This image shows flooding outside the carriage works in Holgate Road. The crowds in the distance are waiting for rescue transport on the corner of Poppleton Road. The second picture shows the flooding in Walker Street that same year. Flooding often damaged several streets behind Marygate and they were condemned and demolished in the 1970s; four terraced streets: Bean, Hetherton, Clayton and Walker Street were cleared to create Marygate car park.

Flooding in Lower Wesley Place, February 1933. Lower Wesley Place was dangerously close to the River Foss; in fact Wray's Yard and Lower Wesley Place extended down to the water's edge; in the 19th century it was an open sewer subject to frequent flooding. One man tried hard to do something about the abject poverty in the area. Benjamin Seebohm (1871-1954), Seebohm was his mother's German family name, joined Rowntree in 1888; he had graduated in chemistry from Owen's College at the University of Manchester. Among his many achievements was establishing the company's first laboratory in 1897 and appointing the firm's first food chemist, Samuel H. Davies, another Quaker. He is, nevertheless, equally well known for his pioneering work on urban poverty and the plight of the poor in his ground-breaking and influential *Poverty: A Study of Town Life*, a book which helped lay the foundations for the modern welfare state. A friend of David Lloyd George's, he is credited with informing the Old Age Pensions Act (1908) and the National Insurance Act (1911). His later works included *Poverty and Progress* (1941) and *Poverty and the Welfare State* (1951).

Hungate residents enyoying the Centenary Celebrations of York Adult Schools, 13th October 1907. In his landmark work, *Poverty*, Seebohm Rowntree describes Hungate as typical of urban slum life: 'reckless expenditure of money as soon as obtained, with the aggravated want at other times; the rowdy Saturday night, the Monday morning pilgrimage to the pawn shop…the despair of so many social workers'.

Nos. 5 and 6 Hill's Yard in the 1930s. Hungate derives from Hundgate – street of the dogs – a common Viking street name. As a result of Seebohm Rowntree's *Poverty*, in 1908 and 1914 York's medical officer, Edmund Smith, produced reports condemning streets in Hungate and Walmgate as unfit for habitation; 'The back yards in Hope Street and Albert Street and in some other quarters can only be viewed with repulsion – they are so small and fetid, and so hemmed-in by surrounding houses and other buildings… There are no amenities; it is an absolute slum.' At the 1921 census York's population was 84,052 with 18,608 inhabited houses (= 4.5 persons per dwelling).

Members of Monkgate Chapel's congregation. In 1903 the Primitive Methodists purchased and opened this new chapel, the location of which was influenced by its closeness to Elmfield College on the Malton Road in Heworth. It offered sittings for 775 persons; at the rear were school premises, including a lecture room, infants room, and assembly hall, with accommodation in total for 600 persons. The organ from Ebenezer Chapel was rebuilt and installed, and special seating with separate entrances was provided for the pupils of Elmfield College. The chapel is also known as John Petty Memorial Chapel, dedicated as it is to the memory of John Petty, first governor of Elmfield College.

St. Stephen's Orphanage children. The orphanage was founded in the 1870s originally in Precentor's Court, moving to Trinity Lane and then to the Mount in 1919; it closed in 1969. Its aim was to accommodate and educate poor girls who had lost one or both parents. The orphanage owned a holiday house in Filey. *Image courtesy of YAYAS and the Evelyn Collection*.

Girls from St. Stephen's Orphanage enjoying themselves on a day trip to Filey in July 1919. *Image courtesy of York Press*.

Highwayman Dick Turpin, also known as John Palmer, was hanged (somewhat fittingly) on the Knavesmire in 1739, for horse stealing – 'a crime worthy of death'. Turpin spent his last six months in the Debtors' Prison, which was built in 1701-05 and is now part of the Castle Museum; the other half of the museum was originally the Female Prison, built in 1780-83. The museum, which opened in 1938, is named after York Castle, which originally stood on the site. Turpin had many visitors: his jailer is said to have earned £100 from selling drinks to Turpin and his guests; Turpin bought a new frock coat and shoes and hired five mourners for £3.10s for the occasion. A report in *The Gentleman's Magazine* for 7th April 1739 notes Turpin's arrogance: 'Turpin behaved in an undaunted manner; as he mounted the ladder, feeling his right leg tremble, he spoke a few

words to the topsman, then threw himself off, and expir'd in five minutes'. The short drop method of hanging meant that those executed were killed by slow strangulation: Turpin was left hanging until late afternoon, before being cut down and taken to The Blue Boar Inn in Castlegate. Turpin's grave in St. George's churchyard was dug particularly deep to deter body snatchers; to no avail: the corpse was removed and found later at the back of Stonegate in a surgeon's garden. Before reburial the coffin was filled with lime. Black Bess, Turpin's steed, was an elaboration added later by writers such as William Harrison Ainsworth in *Rockwood* (1878) and Eliza Cook in her *Black Bess* (1869), an interesting line from which reads: 'And the fame of Dick Turpin had been something less If he'd ne'er rode to York on his bonnie Black Bess'.

University of York: Langwith College. The first petition for a university in York was to King James I in 1617 followed by other unsuccessful attempts in the 18th century, one to annex it to the existing medical school. In 1903 F. J. Munby and others (including the Yorkshire Philosophical Society) proposed a 'Victoria University of Yorkshire'. What was then the College of Ripon and York St. John considered purchasing Heslington Hall as part of a proposed new campus. The campus lake is the largest plastic-bottomed lake in Europe and attracts many waterfowl; the campus also supports a large rabbit population, the hunting of which by students is strictly prohibited. Heslington Hall is a fine Elizabethan manor built by Thomas Eymes in 1568; Eymes was secretary to Henry VIII's Great Council of the North which had its headquarters in King's Manor; as with other buildings of the time, it was constructed in the shape of an 'E', in honour of Queen Elizabeth I. York's first two Colleges, Derwent and Langwith were founded in 1965, and were followed by Alcuin and Vanbrugh in 1967 and Goodricke in 1968. In 1972 Wentworth College opened.

The Chapter House. This octagonal building in between the Minster and St. William's College was completed in 1286 and was the meeting place for the Dean and Chapter. It was designed to emphasise the equality implicit in these two offices: this explains the seats around the edge – not in the middle – and the poor acoustics which meant that anyone speaking from the centre could barely be heard on the perimeter. The rich variety of carvings are said to represent characters from the masons' own lives.

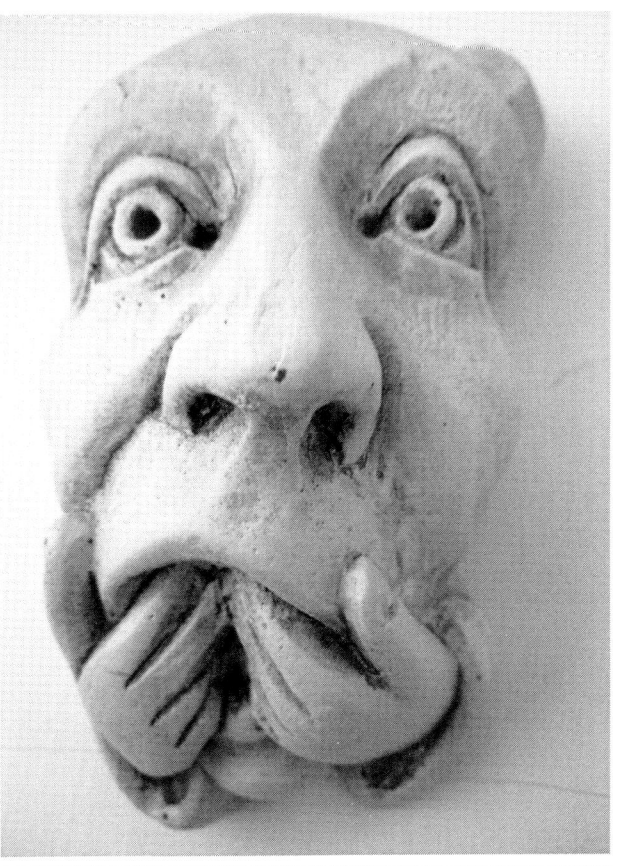

Waiting in the Minster Stoneyard to be incorporated into the Minster stonework.

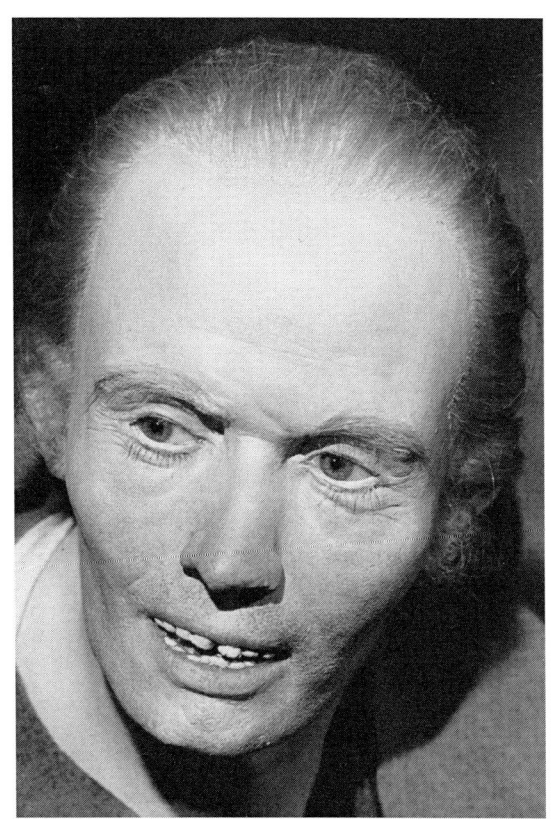

One of the vivid reconstructions which has come out of the Viking excavations is Eymund in the Jorvik Viking exhibit who was born about AD 948 and is reconstructed from a male skeleton unearthed in a Viking cemetery in Fishergate. The only significant archaeological finds in York before the 1970s were dug up by chance, but this all changed when an area below Lloyds Bank in Pavement was excavated by York Archaeological Trust before the redevelopment of Coppergate in 1976: within days rare traces of Viking Age timber buildings were revealed. The dig covered 1,000 square metres and so between 1976 and 1981 archaeologists were able to excavate 2,000 years of York's history. In that time York Archaeological Trust identified and recorded around 40,000 items. The site revealed: five tons of animal bones – mostly food leftovers consumed over the centuries; vast quantities of oyster shells – a cheap and popular food over the years; thousands of Roman and mediaeval roof tiles; building materials including wattle, timber and metal slag; 250,000 pieces of pottery; 20,000 other individually interesting objects. Many of the Viking artefacts are on display here along with a vibrant reconstruction of Viking life. © *York Press*

Men of the Arab Legion at the 1955 Northern Command Military Tattoo; who knows what the old lady thought of it all? Picture reproduced courtesy of *The Press*, York.

York was nothing if not well served by hospitals in the Middle Ages, with at least thirty-one. The most important, and biggest, was St. Leonard's. One of the earliest was St. Nicholas' leper hospital. St. Giles in Gillygate, was set up before 1274. There was a hospital at Ouse Bridge in the 13th century, a Maison Dieu, originally catering for the poor and lepers. St. Mary's Hospital was in Bootham. York County Hospital opened in a rented house in 1740 in

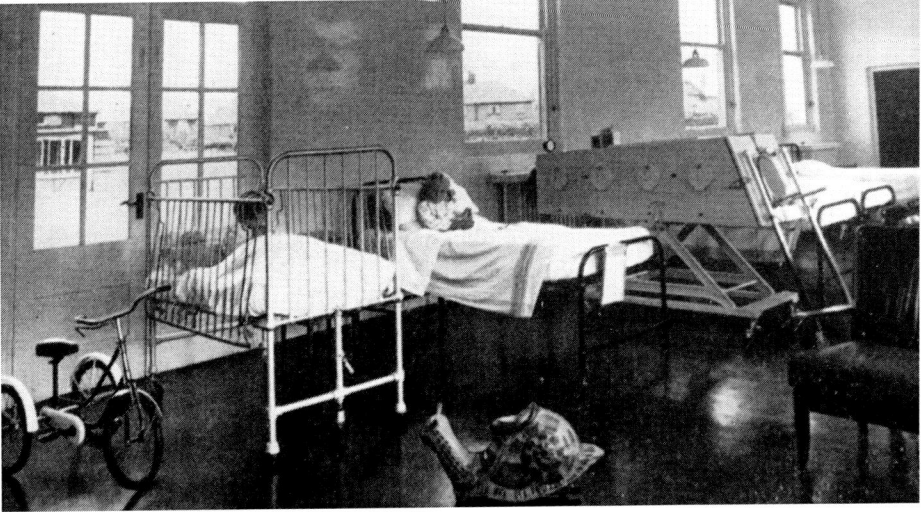

Monkgate. Before that, from 1614, the City Surgeon was responsible for medical care. In 1745 a purpose-built hospital opened on the same site with 50 beds: by 1750 2,417 patients had been treated. As a charitable hospital (where the financiers could choose who received treatment there) the County Hospital was not actually responsible for the city's sick poor; this led to the establishment of the Dispensary. The 18th century also saw the founding of York Lunatic Asylum and the revolutionary Retreat for the care of the mentally ill. The 1745 hospital building was demolished in 1851 and replaced with a new 100 bed hospital costing £11,000. In 1887 it merged with the York Eye Institution, opened in 1875. The present 600 bed York District Hospital opened in 1976 replacing the County Hospital, Fulford Hospital, Deighton Grove Hospital, Yearsley Bridge Hospital, Acomb Hospital, the Military Hospital and City Hospital.

Fulford Open Air School. Originally opened at 11 Castlegate in 1913 in the same building as the Tuberculosis Dispensary, it moved in 1914 to a converted army hut in the grounds of Fulford House and became known as Fulford Road School for Delicate and Partially Sighted Children. The open-air school movement was set up in 1904 in Berlin in the fight against tuberculosis in children and, as such, required the establishment of schools that combined medical care with teaching adapted to pupils with pre-tuberculosis. Fulford closed in 1960 and was demolished in 1964. The Holgate Bridge School for Mentally Defective Boys was opened in 1911 and moved to Fulford House, later known as Fulford Road School for Educationally Sub-Normal Children, in 1923. York had at least four mediaeval leper hospitals, or lazar-houses; in the 1990s York Archaeological trust rediscovered the site of the 1108 Augustinian leper hospital of St. Nicholas in Lawrence Street; excavations uncovered an aisled hall. St. Mary Magdalene was at the end of Bootham just past the Burton Stone; another was near Monkbridge, called St. Leonard or St. Loy. St. Katherine was outside the city beyond Micklegate.

York in the 60s had its own home-grown music scene with venues like the Kavern Club in Micklegate, the Mandrake in Stonegate, and Neil Guppy's Enterprise Club hosting live music by young city bands. Some of it started in the 50s, but much of it persisted throughout the 60s or originated in that decade. The Kavern Club (above and below) started life as a coffee bar in the basement of the Labour Party headquarters, appropriately decorated with graffiti. By 1964 there were 100 or so local groups performing in the city: allegedly, the crime rate fell because most young people were either performing in groups or watching them. © *York Press*

Marooned in Wray's Yard flooding.

SHORTAGE OF COAL.

YORK DEAF AND DUMB MEMBERS PRESENTING LUMPS OF COALS TO THEIR MISSION ROOM

York Deaf & Dumb members presenting coal to their mission room during a shortage in 1919.

River Foss Downstream 1889. In 1069 William the Conqueror dammed the River Foss near to its confluence with the Ouse to create a moat around the castle; this caused the river to flood upstream and form a large lake known as the King's Pool or the King's Fish Pond. King's Pool was an integral feature of the city's inner defences during the Middle Ages – the marsh was virtually impassable and explains why there is no city wall between Layerthorpe Postern and the Red Tower. Roman jetties, wharves and warehouses have been excavated on the river banks, indicating that water-borne transport and trade was important from Roman times. Foss Bridge, at the end of

Walmgate, dates from 1811 and replaces a 1403 stone bridge and a wooden one before that. The fish shambles was here as was the Saturday pig market (the tethering rings still exist) and the goose fair. There was a chicory works near Jewbury which processed the chicory which grew to the north east of the city. The River Foss was canalised by the Foss Navigation Company as far as the bridge at Sheriff Hutton in 1806, a thriving town then. It cost £35,000; 1809 provided the best toll receipts: £1,384. Up cargoes included lime for the local agricultural industry and other materials for the tannery in Strensall, and coal. Goods coming back to York were hay, oats, cheeses, manure and other agricultural produce. The horses that hauled the barges could manage a weight of 27 tons given a favourable current; the same horse could cope with only one ton road cargo. The opening of the York to Scarborough railway through Haxby and Strensall in 1845 and the York to Hull line through Huntington in 1847 rendered the canal commercially redundant in 1852 – the first navigation to close as a result of the railways.

A policeman tries to buy black market King Crimson tickets from York University students in the early 70s. Just look at those loons! *Photo courtesy of York University.*

Bootham Bar (originally Buthum which means at the booths and signifies the markets which used to be held here) stands on the north western gateway of the Roman fortress and was originally called Galmanlith. A door knocker was added to the Bar in 1501 for the use of Scotsmen (and others presumably) seeking admission to the city. The barbican came down in 1831 and the wall steps went up in 1889; a statue of Ebrauk, the pre-Roman founder of York, once stood nearby. Thomas Mowbray's severed head was stuck here in 1405 and the Earl of Manchester bombarded the Bar in 1644 during the Civil war. The barbican was removed in 1831. The removal of the barbican was due in part to complaints by residents of Clifton: 'not fit for any female of respectability to pass through' on account of the droppings of animals en route to the cattle market and its use as a urinal by pedestrians. The three statues on the top were carved in 1894 and feature a mediaeval mayor, a mason and a knight; the mason is holding a model of the restored Bar.

Right: Micklegate Bar with Howard's Punch Bowl on the right and St. Thomas's Hospital on the corner of Nunnery Lane. In 1851 it was an almshouse 'for aged widows', taking in permanent residents and travellers for food and lodging. Until 1791 these widows had to beg on the streets for four days every year for their alms.

Micklegate Bar was originally called Mickleith which means great gate; the royal arms are those of Edward III; the arch is Norman, the rest 14th century; the side arch was added in 1753. Being on the road to and from London this was the Bar through which royal visitors entered York. Edward IV, Richard III, Henry VII, Margaret Tudor, James I, Charles I (on three Civil War occasions) and James II all passed through. Henry VIII was scheduled to enter here but, in the event, came in through Walmgate Bar. Heads and quarters of traitors were routinely displayed on the top, most famously: Lord Scrope of Mastan in 1415; Sir Henry Percy (Hotspur) after his part in the rebellion against Elizabeth I; Richard Duke of York after the Battle of Wakefield in 1460, prompting Shakespeare to write: "Off with his head and set it on York's gates; so York did overlook the town of York" (Queen Margaret in *Henry VI*); Thomas Percy in 1569 – his head remained there for two years. Removal of heads without permission was, not inappropriately, punishable by beheading – guess where the heads ended up. The last displays were in 1746 after the Jacobite Rebellion at Culloden. The heads of James Mayne and William Connelly remained on the Bar until 1754. The barbican was removed in 1826 to allow a circus access to the city; the east side arch was built in 1827.

Stuck in Micklegate Bar in 1969. This 20 feet long lorry was stuck there for three hours with its load of fertilizer. One witness was reported as saying 'I wouldn't mind if he was a foreigner but he's only come from Malton.' St Thomas's Hospital can be seen in the above photograph next to Micklegate Bar; it was demolished in 1862. In 1851 it was an almshouse 'for aged widows' taking in permanent residents and travellers for food and lodging. The Punch Bowl (originally next door) stands on the site now, indicative, like the pub of the same name in Stonegate, of the vogue for drinking punch from the end of the 17th century. As a new, fashionable drink it caught on amongst the Whigs leading to the sign of the punchbowl denoting inns patronised by Whigs. © *York Press*.

Ouse Bridge. The Grand Opera House can be seen in the background (top right). The buildings that today house the Grand Opera House were never intended to be a theatre. The tall section was built as York's Corn Exchange in 1868 with plans to use it occasionally as a concert hall. The auditorium was originally a warehouse opening onto King's Street. In 1902 when the Corn Exchange failed, the buildings were converted by William Peacock. The theatre opened on January 20th 1902 with *Little Red Riding Hood* starring Florrie Ford. In 1903 the name was changed to The Grand Opera House and Empire because new regulations banned smoking in theatres but permitted it in music halls. It stayed with William Peacock's family until 1945; performers included Charlie and Sydney Chaplin, Gracie Fields, Lillie Langtry, George Robey, Cecily Courtneidge and Jimmy Jewel. From 1945-56 F.J. Butterworth owned the theatre and stars such as Vera Lynn, Laurel and Hardy and Morecambe and Wise appeared. In 1958 Shepherd of the Shambles bought it, and it became the SS Empire. The stage, lower boxes and raked stall floor were removed and replaced by a large flat floor suitable for roller-skating, dancing, bingo and wrestling. In 1987 new owners the India Pru Co. Ltd spent £4,000,000 restoring it to its former glory.

King's Staith Looking Towards Ouse Bridge. 'The fairest arch in England'. The very first bridge to span the Ouse was built by the Romans at the end of what is now Stonegate; the Vikings replaced this in 850 with their wooden bridge. This collapsed in 1154 under the weight of spectators congregating to see the return of St. William of York from exile in Sicily after his reinstatement. William made the sign of the cross on seeing the calamity unfold: no one died (one horse suffered a broken leg) and the event was immediately declared a miracle. This bridge was replaced by a stone bridge, part of which was swept away by floods in 1564-65. The new central arch spanned 81 feet; Defoe, in his *Tour Through the Whole Island of Great Britain* soberly described it as 'near 70 foot in diameter; it is, without exception, the greatest in England, some say it's as large as the Rialto at Venice, though I think not.' There were about 50 shops, a prison or kidcote, a town hall and a hospital on the bridge and from 1367 England's first public toilets are reputed to have opened here (issuing into the river): 'the place on Owsbridge callyd the pyssing howes'. Agnes Gretehede was paid two shillings a year to keep them clean in 1544. The present Ouse Bridge was built between 1810 and 1821.

The City Walls were built in the 13th and 14th century on a rampart dating from the 9th and 11th centuries. They survive for the best part of their two miles plus length as do the four Bars and 37 internal towers. Four of the six posterns and nine other towers are lost or have been rebuilt. The walls for the most part are six foot wide and thirteen foot high. They were breached in two places in the 1840s to allow access to York's second railway station and to a goods depot known as the Sack Warehouse.

Wilkie Collins (1824-89), a frequent visitor to York, set his 1862 novel, *No Name*, in the city describing a walk along the walls by Captain Wragge as 'one of the most striking scenes which England can show…the majestic west front of York Minster soared over the city and caught the last brightest light of heaven on the summits of its lofty towers'.

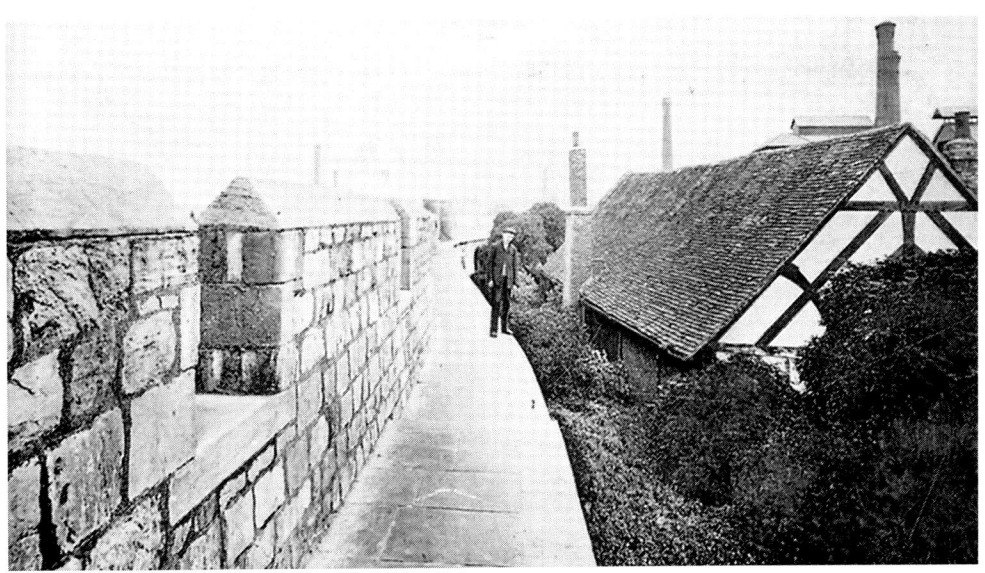

Walmgate Bar, originally known as Walbesgate, is the only York Bar with its barbican intact, thanks largely to William Etty RA who campaigned tirelessly for its preservation. In 1489 it was set on fire by rebels and then bombarded in the Civil War. The inner facade is 16th century and still retains its Doric and Ionic columns. The Rose and Crown can be seen on the right in Lawrence Street. This was a former Tetley Ale House that had its own brewery. Originally, it was two amalgamated houses. Further down towards the Bar is The Waggon and Horses, originally known as the Waggon and, from 1795, the Waggon & Horses. On the other side of the road is The Rook & Gaskill. Messrs Peter Rook and Leonard Gaskill were sheep rustlers from Beverley, who on May 1st 1776, became the last two men to be hanged at the St. Leonard's Gallows at Greendykes in York. Their crime was stealing thirteen sheep from John Brown of Driffield. The pub was previously called the Wheatsheaf, the Princess Victoria in 1834 and then the Queen's Head or the Queen Victoria in 1843. In 1847 it was the Queen Inn. It changed again in 2002 when York Brewery refitted and renamed it to chime with the gallows theme of its first two pubs: The Last Drop Inn and The Three Legged Mare.

Quaint Corners York, Walmgate Bar.

Necessary to provide access to the new railway, Lendal Bridge was opened in 1863 to replace the ferry which plied between the Lendal and Barker Towers. Jon Leeman was the last ferryman – he received £15 and a horse and cart in redundancy compensation. The arrival of the railways had exerted considerable pressure on the ferry service and after considerable argument between the Corporation of York and the railway companies the York Improvement Act was passed in 1860 to allow construction of the first Lendal Bridge. It was designed by the aptly named William Dredge. Unfortunately, this bridge collapsed during construction killing five men; it was replaced by the present bridge, designed by Thomas Page who was responsible also for Skeldergate Bridge here and Westminster Bridge. The remnants of Dredge's bridge were dredged up from the river and sold to Scarborough Council who used the remnants in the construction of Valley Bridge. The factory in the background was Rowntrees' first premises; it was up for sale because the firm had moved to their Haxby Road site.

Skeldergate Bridge: The Drawbridge. The castle-like building here was a toll house; the fee to cross, up to when tolls were ended, was ½d. Work on the bridge began in 1875; it opened in 1881 at a cost of £56,000 – 40% over budget, replacing the ferry which was used by around 800 people each day. The architect, Thomas Page, also designed Lendal Bridge and Westminster Bridge. The River Ouse was crucial to York from earliest times, right through the Roman and Viking occupations and the Middle Ages, making York an important port. Evidence of Irish and German boats date from around 1125. Some Stonegate buildings are said to be built with ships' timbers; there is also a fine figurehead in the same street.

Pre-health & safety days on the bridge. 'The original design of the bridge was altered during planning to enable the north-easternmost span of the bridge to open, allowing tall ships to reach the busy quaysides further upstream. The bridge was last opened in 1975 and the winding mechanism has since been removed. Skeldergate Bridge was originally built as a toll bridge. The toll-house, which also housed the winding machinery, still remains. The bridge was formally declared toll-free on 1st April 1914, an event which was greeted so enthusiastically by the citizens of York that a regatta was held to celebrate the occasion' [from http://www.historyofyork.org.uk/themes/victorian/skeldergate-bridge]

GEORGE STREET BAR.

THWAITES. YORK

Fishergate Bar, sometimes called St. George's Bar, is the gateway to Selby; chains ran across the River Foss here to the castle to reinforce York's defences. The bar was blocked in 1489 after rebels damaged it in protest at punitive taxation (fire damage is still visible); it was eventually reopened in 1827 to allow access to the Cattle Market. In Elizabethan times it was a prison for rascals and lunatics. The John Smith's Phoenix Inn brewery can be seen to the right in Long Close Lane. The original name until the mid 1800s was The Labour in Vain. The sign depicted a white woman vigorously scrubbing a black baby in a frantic bid to make it white; her labours, of course, were in vain. The inscription read 'You may wash him and scrub him from morn till night; your labour's in vain, black will never come white'. The building on the left was Falconer's the furnishers.

Monk Bar, built around 1330, was originally called Monkgate Bar; at 63 feet it is the tallest of York's Bars. Designed as a self-contained fortress, assailants had to cross each floor to reach the next flight of stairs, thus exposing themselves to defensive fire. A perfect fortress, the Bar features loopholes (for bows and arrows); gun ports and murder holes from which heavy objects and boiling water might be dropped. The coat of arms is Plantagenet. The Bar was used as a prison in the 16th century for recusant Catholics, and others: in 1588 Robert Walls was imprisoned for 'drawing blood in a fray'. The barbican was removed in the early 1800s. To rent the rooms at the top, one Thomas Pak (Master Mason at the Minster) paid 4s per annum.

The George Hudson Legacy. York's 'Railway King' advised George Stephenson to make all the trains come through York, rather than Leeds. Hudson was Lord Mayor from 1837-39. His use of public money, though worthy, was questionable: he laid on 'an excellent and substantial breakfast' for poor citizens to celebrate Victoria's coronation in 1838 and doled out free food coupons for 14,000 of the 'lower orders'. By 1846 he was involved in railway projects to the tune of £10 million and was elected Tory MP for Sunderland: his companies controlled more than 25% of England's railways. He was chairman of the York, Newcastle and Berwick Railway and, in 1854, the North Eastern Railway, before being disgraced when dubious share dealings were uncovered by George Leeman and others. He was expelled from the city council in 1849 , and his effigy at Madame Tussauds was ignominiously melted down. After a period of exile in Calais he stood for the Whitby parliamentary seat in 1865 (vacant on the death of George Stephenson) but was arrested before the election and jailed for three months at York. He died in London, a pauper, in 1871.

Hudson was prominent in York's development as a major railway city; his advice to George Stephenson was to make it a hub: "Mak all t'railways cum t'York". The first train left York for South Milford in 1839. The first London service was in 1840 via Derby or Birmingham and took about eleven hours. In 1841 the industry in York employed 41 people; this rose to 513 by 1851 (390 of whom were from out of town bringing 537 dependents); by the end of the century NER employed 5,500 workers in York, about half in the carriage works. In the 1850s the railway replaced the five or so stage coaches per day between London and York which started in 1703 (carrying 24,000 passengers per year, 6 per coach, and taking 4-6 days depending on the weather) with 13 trains carrying 341,000 passengers. The fare to London via Grantham in 1882 was 33s 4d (I class), 25s 4d (II class – equal to about 1 week's wages for a semi-skilled man). 15s 8d (III class). By 1888 there were 294 trains arriving at the station each day.

Leaving York in the early '70s.

The laying of electric tram lines in 1910 replaced the horse-drawn trams. In 1900 there had been eleven such trams drawn by horses from a pool of thirty-three. The tram lines were all taken up again in 1935 as car use increased. The last journey from Nessgate on November 16th was witnessed by large crowds gathered at midnight to watch the Lord Mayor and Inspector J. Stewart – the driver of the very first service – drive York trams into oblivion. The electrification cost £89,741; over eight miles of track were laid. The first day of the tram service, January 20th 1910, saw 6,786 passengers carried with fares totalling £35 18s 5d – as the universal fare was 2d there must have been quite a few fare dodgers. Rail cars (as trams were called) plied between Fulford and South Bank; Fulford and Acomb; Haxby Road and South Bank and Haxby Road and Acomb – and vice versa on a ten minute service between 8.00 am and 10.45, plus works specials; 2-10 on Sundays.

York Corporation Accumulator Station charging up the electric trams at Clifton.

A Karrrier-Clough Trolleybus in East Parade in the 1930s. York Corporation Tramways (YCT) ran an electric tramway and trolleybus service in York between 1910 and 1935. The photo shows one of three 32-seat single deck Charles H Roe bodied Karrier-Cloughs purchased, resuming the trolleybus operation on route 4, from the foot of Parliament Street to Heworth in October 1931. The trolleybuses were withdrawn on 5th January 1935.

York has had three railway stations. The first was a temporary wooden building on Queen Street outside the walls, opened in 1839 by the York & North Midland Railway. It was replaced in 1841, on Tanner Row within the walls, by what is now called the old York railway station and was built by Robert Stephenson on land owned by Lady Hewley's Charity almshouses. Scawin's Railway Hotel, opened the same year, was demolished in 1900. The King of Saxony and Charles Dickens were amongst travellers arriving here. The buildings were reminiscent of Euston Station in Euston Square. Access was difficult, from North Street, and this eventually led to the construction of Hudson Street (after George Hudson), and Lendal Bridge. Because through trains between London and Newcastle needed to reverse out of George Hudson's old York Station in order to continue their journey, a new station was built outside the walls, designed by the North Eastern Railway architects Thomas Prosser and William Peachey, which opened in 1877. It had thirteen platforms and was at that time the largest station in the world. At 800 feet long and 234 feet wide this is one of the most spectacular examples of railway architecture in the world, rightly and famously described as 'A splendid monument of extravagance', and 'York's propylaeum'. As part of the new station project, the Royal Station Hotel (now The Principal Hotel), designed by Peachey, opened in 1878. This shows station number two.

York's biggest brewery was the Ebor Brewery founded by Joseph Hunt in 1834; he was registered as a hop and seed merchant at 2 Monk Bar. By 1851 he was brewer, malster, hop, seed & guavo merchant at 20 Aldwark. The Ebor Brewery was established in 1895 and in 1904 took over Robert Brogden, Sons Co. along with their 60 or so licensed pubs. Ebor was acquired by Cameron & Co of what was then West Hartlepool in 1954. Hunt's also had a lemonade bottling plant in Bedern, just round the corner, and it owned the Ebor Vaults public house.

Apparently, the inn served the cheapest beer in York because the barrels were just rolled across the yard and that meant no dray charges. Where there was beer there was occasional philanthropy. The Hunt Memorial Homes in Fulford were a gift to the local community from local brewer, Sir John Hunt, in 1954. There are 24 cottages housing ten couples and fourteen individuals, together with two staff houses for a nurse and a handy-man

The wreck of the *Sir Ralph Wedgwood* at York station after being bombed by the Luftwaffe during the Baedeker raid of April 29th 1942. That same night the roundhouse took a direct hit and all of the twenty engines in there at the time suffered damage. With terrible bad timing the blacked out 10.15 pm express from King's Cross, the *Night Scotsman*, pulled into platform 9 crammed with passengers – military and civilian – worn out after a five hour journey. The loudspeaker urgently warned them to evacuate but few initially did, encumbered in many cases by full kit and weapons. A 250 pound bomb changed all that when it smashed through the station roof exploding on platforms 2 and 3 and destroying the parcels office, and the *Night Scotsman*.

Established in 1885 by the then Dean, the Very Reverend Purey Cust, as a memorial to General Gordon killed in Khartoum in 1884, Military Sunday lasted until 1939 and was hugely popular with some people walking through the night to attend. The official name of York Minster is The Cathedral and Metropolitical Church of St. Peter in York. It is the largest mediaeval building in England and the biggest cathedral in Europe north of the Alps. It towers on the site of an earlier Norman cathedral which was almost as huge and took 250 years to build from 1220 to 1470. Its treasures are countless. They include 128 stained glass windows from the 12th to the 21st century, most notable of which is the 1408 Great East Window – the size of a tennis court – the world's largest area of stained glass. The Minster is built in the shape of a cross, facing east towards Jerusalem.

When is a cathedral not a cathedral? When it is a minster. There is, however, very little distinction between the two. Minsters were originally, from the 7th century, any communal settlement of clergy where the act of prayer was routinely practised. They were later established as missionary teaching, collegiate, churches, or a church attached to a monastery from which monks would go out and preach to the local community; a cathedral, on the other hand was the seat of a bishop, his seat or throne, being a *cathedra*. Examples other than York are at Beverley, Westminster and Southwell. Minsters declined in the 11th century with the rise of the parish church and the name was then bestowed on 'any large or important church, especially a collegiate or cathedral church', like York. The 20th and 21st centuries have seen an explosion in the number of parish churches honoured with the title 'minster'. Hull is a nearby example.

Minster School Match of the Day. There has been choral singing at York for over 1,000 years, beginning with clergy singers, boy choristers for much of that time and lay songmen for around 500 years. The choristers are all students at the neighbouring Minster School aged seven to thirteen. York Minster was one of the UK's first cathedrals to introduce girl choristers alongside the boys; they share the singing of the eight sung services each week equally, joining forces at Christmas and Easter. Lancelot Blackburne (archbishop and pirate) was Archbishop of York from 1724 until his death in 1743, before which he did time as a paid spy of Charles II in 1681, and as a pirate in the Caribbean in the 1680s. He reputedly drank ale and smoked a pipe during confirmations, behaviour typical of the man and described as follows: 'His behaviour was seldom of a standard to be expected of an archbishop…in many respects it was seldom of a standard to be expected of a pirate'.

The Old Palace not only houses York Minster's library and archives but also the Collections Department and the conservation studio. It is known as The Old Palace because part of the building used to be the chapel of the 13th century Archbishop's palace. In 1810 it was refurbished and, shortly after, the Minster's collection was installed there. The original library was the dream and ambition of King Egbert, a disciple of the Venerable Bede: he opened a school of international repute and started a collection of books. The librarianship then passed from 778-781 to Flaccus Albinus Alcuinus, better known as Alcuin. He later become one of the architects of the Carolingian Renaissance. Alcuin's catalogue featured works by many of the Church Fathers and classical authors such as Pliny, Aristotle, Cicero and Virgil – but all was tragically lost when the Minster and library were sacked by the Vikings. It was not until the 18th century that the collection started to grow significantly: from 1716 to 1820, there were more than 1,200 loans by 179 different borrowers. Laurence Sterne, author of *The Life and Opinions of Tristram Shandy, Gentleman* was a regular user. By 1810 there were nearly 8,000 volumes and the library moved to its present home in Dean's Park; in 1890 Edward Hailstone bequeathed 10,000 volumes. Sadly, many books were sold to raise money for repairs, including a 1519 Erasmus' *New Testament* for £20,000; however, the proceeds went to the new Library Fund started in 1945; today it is unquestionably the finest cathedral library in Britain. © *York Press*.

The Deanery. The Old Palace not only houses York Minster's library and archives but also the Collections Department and the conservation studio. It is known as The Old Palace because part of the building used to be the chapel of the 13th century Archbishop's palace. In 1810 it was refurbished and, shortly after, the Minster's collection was installed there.

St. William's College, College Street. Originally the House of the Prior of Hexham it is named after Archbishop William Fitzherbert (St. William) and built in 1465 by order of Warwick the Kingmaker. From about 1890 the 15th century half timbering was covered in stucco; it was removed again in 1906. The college was split into tenements at the time but formerly was home to the Minster's Chantry: 23 priests and their provost.

The central doors were made by Robert Thompson of Kilburn: his trademark mouse can be seen on the right hand door. A rental document of 1845 tells us that annual rents are 32s for five tenements, three cottages (2s each) and one messuage (2s 4d). From 1680-1761 the cottages were variously occupied by a painter, joiner, translator, cordwainer. They were nearly demolished in 1912 to make way for the tramline to Heworth. Frank Green, owner of the nearby Treasurer's House, bought the College and gave it in 1906 to the Convocation of York, whose meeting place it was until the amalgamation of the Convocations of York and Canterbury created the Synod of the Church of England. George Hudson had a draper's store in one of the shops here.

York Castle was established as one of two castles by William I; Henry III rebuilt the castle in 1260 as part of the city defences replacing the wooden Bar walls with stone. The site has housed a prison and the Castle Museum. Clifford's Tower survives. The buildings here make up the 'Eye of the Ridings'. Originally King's Tower, or even the 'Minced Pie', but from 1596 named after Francis Clifford, Earl of Cumberland, who restored it for use as a garrison after it had been partly dismantled by Robert Redhead in 1592. An alternative etymology comes from Roger de Clifford whose body was hung there in

chains in 1322. Built in wood by William the Conqueror when he visited to establish his northern HQ in 1190, it was burnt down when 150 terrified York Jews sought sanctuary here from an anti-semitic mob and many committed suicide or were slaughtered. It was rebuilt in stone by King John and Henry III as a quadrilobate between 1245 and 1259 as a self-contained stronghold and royal residence and housed the kingdom's Treasury in the 14th century. Robert Aske, one of the prime movers in the Pilgrimage of Grace, was hanged here on July 12th 1537. On April 23rd 1684 the roof was blown off during an over-enthusiastic seven gun salute. The motte is 48 feet high and the tower itself 33 feet. The moat was fed by a diversion from the Ouse.

The museum gardens were designed in the 'Gardenesque' style by landscape architect, Sir John Murray Naysmith in the 1830s in four acres formerly known as Manor Shore. They show off the buildings of the museum and abbey at their best while also providing space for displaying plant specimens as a botanical garden. As more and more exotic specimens were introduced, a conservatory was built to house tropical plants such as sugar cane, coffee, tea, ginger and cotton as well as orchids and epiphytes. A pond was created to accommodate a large rare water-lily, the *Victoria amazonica*. Although the pond and the conservatory are long gone, the ten-acre gardens are still a listed botanical garden and contain many varieties of trees, deciduous and evergreen, native and exotic. From 1835 until 1961 an entrance fee was charged. York Swimming Bath Company's pool opened in 1837; it was closed in 1922 and filled in, in 1969.

The Hospitium. This fine 14th century half-timbered building in Museum Gardens was probably designed both as a guest house for visitors to the nearby St. Mary's Abbey and as a warehouse for goods unloaded from the river nearby. There was an Elizabethan knot garden (visible here) with a central fountain between the Hospitium and the river.

The Red House dates from 1718 – its candle snuffer can still be seen; Dr. John Burton (*Tristram Shandy's* Dr. Slop) once lived there; it is now an antiques centre. Burton was a gynaecologist and medical author whose books included *An Essay Towards a Complete System of Midwifery*, illustrated by no less an artist than George Stubbs who had come to York (then, as now, a centre of excellence in medical science) to learn his anatomy. Stubbs found work teaching medical students in the medical school before taking up comparative anatomy, and painting his famous horses. His most celebrated, *Whistlejacket*, was painted in 1762 and featured the horse that won the four mile chase for 2,000 guineas at the Knavesmire in August 1759. Burton, a medical doctor educated at Cambridge, Leiden and Rheims, also authored the unfinished *Monasticon Eboracense*, an ecclesiastical history of Yorkshire in 1758; he was incarcerated in York Castle after his involvement in the 1745 Jacobite Rebellion as 'a suspicious person to His Majesty's government'.

Queen Margaret's Arch is named after Margaret Tudor, who stayed in York in 1503 on her way to marry James IV of Scotland. Adjacent to the Bar Walls opposite the King's Manor, it was built in 1497 as a short cut to and from St Mary's Abbey for use by Henry VII for 'his pleasure and passage to the Mynster'.

The British Workman was a 1d monthly periodical, published by S.W. Partridge and Co in London who were founded by Thomas Bywater Smithies (b. 1817) of York in 1855. It was published between 1855 and 1892, and aimed to "promote the health, wealth and happiness of the working classes". The text, written by a pool of authors, blended socialism and Protestantism. Smithies was a strong advocate of temperance and this was reflected in his paper. No. 57's massive print run of 200,000 was underwritten by four friends with all copies being donated to the London City Mission to be distributed abroad. By 1868 there were editions in four major European languages as well as in Latin. Eminent artists like George Cruikshank (1792-1878) and Sir John Gilbert drew for it and Lord Shaftsbury was a constant supporter. Florence Nightingale distributed it to troops in the Crimean War. Smithies died in 1883.

The King's Manor. This marvellous, often overlooked, building off Exhibition Square, was originally built in 1270 as the house of the Abbott at St. Mary's Abbey. The Wilberforce Memorial was the charity behind the Yorkshire School for the Blind; it was established in the King's Manor on the death of William Wilberforce in 1833 out of a desire to honour his memory and good works in as fitting a manner as possible. Wilberforce had represented Yorkshire as an MP for 28 years and was an influential voice not just for the movement to abolish the slave trade but also for the education and training of the blind. The school's mission was: 'To provide sound education together with instruction in manual training and technical work, for blind pupils, between the ages of five and twenty; to provide employment in suitable workshops or homes for a limited number of blind men and women who've lost their sight after the age of sixteen, in some occupation carried on at the school; and to promote such other agencies for the benefit of the blind as may enable them to gain their livelihood, or spend a happy old age.'

April 28th 1942. The raids on York, Norwich, Bath, Canterbury and Exeter became known as Baedeker because Goering's staff allegedly used the famous travel guide to select their *Vergeltungsangriffe* (retaliatory) targets – namely 3 *** English cities – in retaliation for the RAF destruction of Lubeck and Rostock. Seventy German bombers, largely unopposed, bombed York for two hours: 86 people died including fourteen children, and 98 were seriously injured (not including undisclosed army and RAF fatalities). 9,500 houses (30% of the city's stock) were damaged or destroyed leaving 2,000 people homeless. The Guildhall (shown here) and St. Martin le Grand Church were badly damaged.

The Bar Convent is the oldest lived-in convent in England. It was established as a school for Catholic girls in 1686 by Frances Bedingfield, an early member of Mary Ward's Institute, in response to Sir Thomas Gascoigne's demand: 'We must have a school for our daughters'. Sir Thomas, a local Catholic landowner, provided £450 to set up a boarding school; this was followed in 1699 by a free day school. For Catholics the 17th century was often a time of persecution and the Bar Convent was very much a clandestine community. Known as the 'Ladies at the Bar' the sisters wore plain grey day dresses rather than habits to avoid raising suspicion. April 1769 saw the first Mass held in the beautiful new chapel, with its magnificent, but externally unobtrusive, neo-classical dome concealed beneath a pitched slate roof.

In 'Two hours of intense bombing and machine-gunning', the Bar Convent School collapsed killing five nuns including the headmistress, Mother Vincent. The following day the *Daily Mail* reported: 'The gates of York still stand high, like the spirit of its people who, after nearly two hours of intense bombing and machine-gunning, were clearing up today". There is a plaque on York Railway Station in honour of Station Foreman William Milner who died in the raid while entering a burning building to get medical supplies. His body was found still holding the box; he was posthumously awarded the King's Commendation for Gallantry.

Opened, or rather closed, in 1961 this piece of Cold War furniture was officially No. 20 Group Royal Observer HQ operated by UKWMO, the UK Warning and Monitoring Organisation. Its role was to function as one of 29 monitoring and listening posts in the event of a nuclear explosion. Decommissioned in 1991, English Heritage have opened this Cold War bunker to the public to enable them to see the decontamination areas, living quarters, communications centre and operations rooms.

Parts of Barley Hall go back as far as 1360, when it was built as the York town house for Nostell Priory, the Augustinian monastery near Wakefield, by Thomas de Dereford, the Prior from 1337 to 1372. The Priors of Nostell were prebendary canons of York Minster and attended ceremonies, services and business meetings in the city; a hostel, therefore, made good commercial sense. However, by the 15th century, the Priory had fallen on hard times and Barley Hall was leased out to private tenants. A new wing was added in about 1430 and in 1460 it was rented out to William Snawsell – goldsmith, Master of the Royal Mint in York, MP for York, Alderman and Lord Mayor of York in 1468. By the 17th century it was subdivided into a number of smaller dwellings so that the 'screens passage' – the internal corridor area at the end of the Great Hall – came to be used as a public short-cut through from Stonegate to Swinegate. To this day it remains a public right-of-way, known as Coffee Yard . By Victorian times, the house was 'a warren of tradesmen's workshops' and its last use before being sold for redevelopment in 1984 was as a plumber's workshop and showroom. The Hall was painstakingly restored to its former glory and it re-opened to the public in 1993. Barley Hall is named after Professor Maurice Barley, founder president of York Archaeological Trust.

The Picture House, Coney Street, opened in 1915.

By 1919 York had no shortage of picture houses; popularity continued to grow and in the 1940s they included The Picture House, Coney Street; The Tower in New Street (so small it only had four rows in the balcony); St. George's in 1921 (next to Fairfax House). The Electric opened in Fossgate in 1911, renamed the Scala in 1951 where the entrance was through a door beneath the screen. It closed in 1957 and became a furniture shop and is now a café-restaurant; the exterior is beautifully preserved. Locally it was known as the 'Flea Bin' – and a visit meant a 'laugh and scratch'. Admission on Saturday afternoon was 4d – or a clean jam jar. The Regent (Acomb); the Grand (Clarence St. from 1919); the 1937 Odeon in Blossom Street and the art deco Clifton; the Rialto in Fishergate – formerly the Casino and the City Picture Palace in 1914; it promoted itself as offering 'World Famous artists of Radio, Stage, Screen and Concert Platform; World Famous Orchestras' as well as 'World Famous Films'. The Clifton (cinema and ballroom) was the first in York to have an organ that rose up in front of the screen; its first film was *Sabu the Elephant Boy*. The first to open, though, was the converted Wesleyan Chapel known as the New Street Palace of Varieties which opened in 1909 with a film showing the Messina earthquake and tsunami of 1908.

The Grand Picture House opened on 10th November 1919 in Clarence Street with Lily Else in *Comradeship*. There was a ballroom on the first floor and a café on the ground floor. The picture house closed on 1st February 1958 with Alan Ladd in *The Gun Runner*. The ballroom continued as Christie's Ballroom until demolition in 1989. The Odeon opened in 1937 in Blossom Street on the site of the Crescent Café & Dance Salon typical of Oscar Deutsch's Art Deco 'palaces for the people'. They were intended to evoke luxury liners and to exude luxury in contrast to the ordinariness found in most pre-war homes. A Union Jack flew from the roof whenever a British film was showing. The opening ceremony was celebrated by flags and bunting stretching to Micklegate Bar while the Odeon was lit by neon lights and a spotlight to illuminate the whole of Blossom Street. VIP guests included Viscount and Viscountess Milton as well as Oscar Deutsch and all 1,484 seats had sold out within 90 minutes; the first person in the queue was presented with a bottle of champagne. Odeon derives from 'Oscar Deutsch Entertains our Nation?' Not a bit of it: the Odeons were named after the ancient Greek for a building used for a musical performance.

Images from the Evelyn Collection, courtesy of YAYAS.

The Crescent Café & Danse Salon opened in 1925 in Blossom Street.

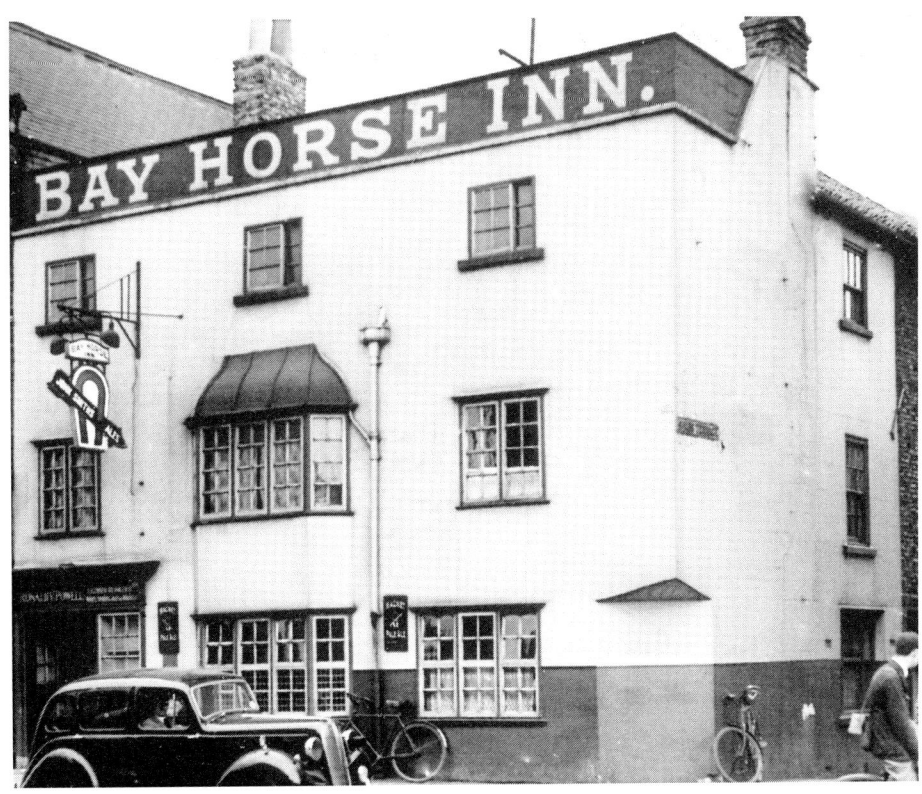

The Bay Horse in Blossom Street, seen here in 1940, is a 17th century pub with unspoilt interior: sloping floors, big beams and original fireplaces make this a traditional English pub that also had a brewhouse. The pub dates back more than 265 years, and occupies a key spot on one of the busiest routes into the city centre. Controversy rages over whether this Bay Horse or The Bay Horse (now Keystones) in Monkgate were once called The Bay Malton, named after a horse which flourished between 1764 and 1767. In 1861 Richard Cowper, professional horse breaker, was licensee; he sold out to the Institute of the Blessed Virgin Mary.

Botterill's Repository for Horses was built in 1884 next to Lendal Bridge and was reduced in height by a half in 1965 when it became a car dealers. Patrick Nuttgens described the original building as 'an exotic red and yellow Byzantine building with ramps inside, up which the horses were led to their stalls – a kind of multi-storey horse car park'. It was frequently used by patrons of the 1868 Yorkshire Club for Gentlemen (River House) in from the country, just over Lendal Bridge. The pub to the left is the Lendal Bridge; it was originally called the Railway Tavern (because it was near York's two railway stations) when established in 1842. The current owner purchased the pub from Bass in 1992, and renamed it The Maltings.

One of the finest Georgian town houses in England, Fairfax House was originally the winter home of Viscount Fairfax having been purchased in 1760 as a dowry to Anne Fairfax. Its richly decorated interior was redesigned in the classical style by York architect John Carr with a magnificent staircase, ceilings, Venetian window and iron balusters. Adapted in the last century for use as a cinema and dance hall, Fairfax House was restored to its former glory by York Civic Trust in 1982-84. Sir Simon Jenkins said of it in 2003 'it is the most perfect eighteenth century townhouse I have come across anywhere in England.' The Noel Terry collection of furniture, clocks, paintings and decorative arts, described by Christie's as one of the finest private collections of the 20th century, furnish the house.

Between 1370 and 1879 564 convicts were either beheaded or hanged at York's Knavesmire (where the racecourse is today), or Tyburn. Executions were held on the Knavesmire until 1802 when the Grand Jury decided that the 'entrance to the town should no longer be annoyed by dragging criminals through the streets'; the gallows were then transferred to the Castle (The New Drop) and then, in 1868, to a scaffold within the prison nearby. Dick Turpin is, of course, the most notorious Knavesmire, or Tyburn, victim. Duke 'Butcher' Cumberland on his victorious return from bloody Culloden left a number of prisoners here to show his gratitude for the city's hospitality: the Sheriff's chaplain read out the message: 'And the Lord said unto Moses "Take all the heads of the people and hang them up before the sun"'. Twenty-three were duly left to hang for ten minutes, stripped and quartered, their heads stuck on Micklegate Bar. Cumberland Street was named after the butcher Duke.

York Races in 1972.

The Ebor Meeting of 1908.

The Knavesmire. Grazing horses and cattle were a common sight on the Knavesmire from the early 19th century through to the 1960s, originally because local householders held grazing rights here and because grazing was the traditional way of managing the pasture. York Races moved to the Knavesmire in 1731 from flood-prone Clifton, sometimes attracting crowds of over 100,000. The races were accompanied by side shows, gypsy bands and cock fights, and executions at York's Tyburn.

The steward's box, 1955. © *York Press.*

St. George's Field was home to the York ducking stool – for scoundrels and women who sold short measures or bad beer and 'scolds and flyters'. The gallows nearby attracted large crowds, some coming by special train excursions as late as 1862. There were heated baths here from 1879 to 1972: they comprised separate men's and women's baths and a bath for York residents without a bath at home.

Foam and tonic baths were installed at St. George's Baths Building in 1935; they were reputed to be effective against rheumatism and obesity. Cost was 2s 6d for 20 minutes. Hot air is forced into a hot bath followed by a squeeze of Zotofoam providing a body massasge to 'eliminate unwanted secretions from the pores of the skin'. Dubbed as a jacuzzi on steroids they were popular until the 1960s.

York Theatre Royal. The first theatre was built on tennis courts in Minster Yard in 1734 by Thomas Keregan. In 1744 his widow built The New Theatre here on what was the city's Mint, itself built on the site of St. Leonard's Hospital. In 1765 it was rebuilt by Joseph Baker and enlarged to seat 550, 'by far the most spacious in Great Britain, Drury Lane and Covent Garden excepted', according to the *York Courant*. Access to the site of the Mint can still be gained from the back of the main stage. At this time the theatre was illegal and it was not until a Royal Patent was granted in 1769 and the theatre was renamed the Theatre Royal that this status changed. Gas lighting came in 1824 and in 1835 a new frontage was built facing onto the newly-created St. Leonard's Place. © *York Press*.

The York & Ainsty Hounds Meet at Clifton. The Wapentake (a subdivision of a county) of Ainsty (taking in 35 townships) lay largely to the west of the city of York between the Rivers Ouse, Wharfe and Nidd and was named after Ainsty Cliff near Bilborough which in turn is named after the Roman road which ran nearby.

The City Roller Skating Palace. By the start of the First World War this had become the City Picture Palace cinema on Fishergate – which was itself later to become the Casino and eventually the Rialto.

Pavement Vaults (1942) and its earlier incarnations are steeped in history. It was trading as the Board in the 1880s when brewers J.J. Hunt bought the premises and business of William Cooper, wine and spirit merchant. The 'unsightly old property' was replaced in 1893 with a new jettied and pargeted building, resplendent with a Burmantoft ware entrance hall. Originally, it was on Pavement, a medieval street dating back to 1378, but was wrecked in order to make way for Piccadilly. Prior to the demolition the site was a coaching inn. The White Swan Hotel was built on the site 1912 and the 'Centre Bar', housed within the hotel, was 'a popular hangout for York's young hedonists', whatever they were. The hotel finally closed in 1982 but reopened in 2017 under its former Pavement Vaults name.

The Mystery Plays were revived during the 1951 York Festival of the Arts and were performed on a fixed stage in the Museum Gardens – it was not until 1954 that a wagon play, *The Flood*, toured the streets. The 1951 production was the most popular Festival of Britain event in the country, with over 26,000 people seeing the plays. The word 'mystery' in this context means a 'trade' or 'craft' in mediaeval English; it is also, of course, a religious truth or rite. The mediaeval plays were traditionally sponsored by the city's craft guilds. Nowadays, the mediaeval Corpus Christi plays are produced every four years, most recently in 2018, by the York Guilds and Companies. *The Creation* to the *Last Judgement* is paraded through the streets on pageant wagons as actors perform selections from the 48 high points of Christian history at twelve playing stations designated by the city banners with one guild taking responsibility for one episode. The sole surviving manuscript of the York plays, from around 1465, is in the British Library.

Parliament Street Market around 1920 and 1964. The street is named after the Act of Parliament of 1833 which allowed for the market here.

The Commercial Academy was established by Mr. Randall in the Thursday Market Hall, now St. Sampson's Square, in 1748. The curriculum was nothing if not progressive and included: The Best English Authors; the Italian Method of Bookkeeping; the Terrestrial Globe Considered as a Map of the World with the Astronomical Parts of Geography.

Gillygate was originally called 'Invico Sancti Egidi', then Giligate in 1373 after St. Giles Church. The church was demolished in 1547; the Salvation Army citadel opened by General Booth in 1882 now stands on the site but is closed. Clarence Street houses and nearby Union Street car park were built on land which in 1835 was called the Horsefair as three horse fairs were held here every year.

Goodramgate is named after Guthrum, a Danish chief active around 878. In 1901 York Minster gave permission for Deangate to pass close to the South Transept, linking Goodramgate with Duncombe Place and High Petergate. In time this led to over 2,000 vehicles per hour passing close to the Minster. It was closed to traffic in 1991. The pub on the left in the upper photo is the Golden Slipper.

The Grade I listed Lady Row cottages (Nos. 60-72) date from 1316. They are the oldest surviving jettied cottages in Britain. Originally nine or ten houses for the priests at neighbouring Holy Trinity Church, the one at the southern end was demolished in 1766 to make way for a gateway to the 13th-15th century Holy Trinity Church. They each comprised one room ten by fifteen feet on each floor. Rents collected went to pay for chantries to the blessed Virgin Mary in nearby churches. Two pubs occupied the cottages at various times: The Hawk's Crest from 1796-1819 and The Noah's Ark around 1878.

Low Petergate follows the route of the Roman *Via Principalis* and is named after the Minster. York College for Girls was established in 1908 at 62 Low Petergate in a fine building that is, in parts, at least 300 years old; it closed in 1997 and is now an Italian restaurant. The first headmistress had the nickname E3, derived from her initials – Elizabeth Emma Ellett. Former pupils include Dame Janet Baker, OBE.

York's best bookshop, The Little Apple, is in High Petergate. Fiona Mozley, author of 2017 Booker short-listed *Elmet* works here; she has also won the 2018 Somerset Maugham Award. Further down is the Eagle & Child; built in 1640, the Grade II* listed timber-framed pub is a Leeds Brewery house converted in November 2015 from the building previously occupied by Plunkets restaurant since 1977. The building is reputed to have once been owned by the Terry family of chocolate fame and is famous for the graffiti scrawled on the upstairs bar wall in lipstick by the five original members of the Rolling Stones when it was a coffee bar called Pete Maddens. The Stones were in there after a concert in Leeds in 1968. The autographed wall has been preserved for posterity.

Stonegate is by common consent one of the finest streets in England, if not Europe, and York's first 'foot-street', pedestrianised in 1971 and paving the way for many more. Stonegate was once famous for its coffee shops (hence Coffee Yard). The old Roman stone paving – hence the name – survives under the cobbles complete with the central gulley for the chariots' skid wheels. It was the Roman *Via Praetoria*.

The Norman House is an often overlooked treasure in the yard of 52 Stonegate. It is the oldest domestic building in York and was very large, obviously owned by a man of some wealth and taste. Ye Olde Starre Inne is York's oldest licensed public house, serving us since at least 1644. The striking gallows sign of the Olde Starre Inne still stretches across the street – originally erected in 1733 by landlord Thomas Bulmer who was obliged to pay the owner of the building over the street on to which it joined – 5s rent per year. In 1886 it read 'Boddy's Star Inn'; the pub is named after Charles I – popularly known as 'the Old Star' and was used as a Civil War morgue, field station and operating theatre by the Parliamentarians, much to the disgust of the Royalist landlord. The cellar is 10th century and the well was once the only source of clean water in the area.

This elegant street was originally called Galman and extended from Bootham Bar to Marygate. No. 49 was lived in by Joseph Rowntree; called Lady Armstrong's Mansion it cost £4,500 and included six acres of land; it was later taken over by Bootham School. W.H. Auden's house was opposite. Wystan Hugh Auden was born at No. 54, Bootham on February 21st 1907; his father, G.A. Auden, was Medical Officer for York and author of *The Gild of Barber Surgeons of the City of York*.

Gillygate and Bootham.

Bootham, 1898 N H Excursion by H Pumphrey.

The Lunatic Asylum, Bootham, built to John Carr's design, opened in 1777 with fifteen patients rising to 199 by 1813; its mission was to be caring 'without undue severity'. Part of the asylum burnt down in 1814 with the tragic loss of four patients, and patient records; somewhat convenient, perhaps, as the fire coincided with allegations aimed at the management of the asylum, and with the rise of the Retreat, a very different type of psychiatric hospital. All staff were dismissed and replaced. In the same year a visiting magistrate had reported that the 'house is yet in a shocking state…a number of secret cells in a state of filth horrible beyond description' and the floor covered 'with straw perfectly soaked with urine and excrement'. The asylum advertised that, 'patients are admitted according to their circumstances, the terms for pauper patients belonging to the City, Ainsty and County are 8 shillings per week'. In 1904 it was renamed Bootham Park Hospital. In 1777, it was only the fifth purpose-built asylum in the country. One of the founders was Dr. Alexander Hunter, the hospital's only physician for many years. His publications include *The Medical History of Worms*.

Coney Street in the 1940s. The earliest record of the name is in 1213 when it was called Cuningstreta, from the Viking word *konungra* for king and *straet* (street). Later writers refer to it as Cunny Street. So, it was, and is, King's street. Leak & Thorp's was built on the site of the 14th century Old George Inn, demolished in 1869. The clock outside St. Martin Le Grand church dates from 1668; it was damaged in the Baedeker Raid; restored in 1966 (complete with the 'Little Admiral' with sextant who survived the raid) it is still telling us the time of day.

The George Hotel was one of York's coaching inns serving Hull, Manchester and Newcastle in Coney Street opposite the Black Swan and the York Courant until 1869 when the inn was tragically knocked down to make way for Leak & Thorp, seen here in the 1950s. In 1867 it was called Winn's George Hotel. There was an earlier inn on the site called The Bull: the landlord, Thomas Kaye, replaced this with The George in 1614. Famous guests included Anne and Charlotte Bronte in May 1849 en route to Scarborough; they shopped and visited the Minster. Four days later Anne died of consumption aged twenty-nine.

Fire in Coney Street. In 1933 a devastating fire almost brought one store to its knees, but it recovered, just, and eventually resumed its role as one of the premier department stores in the north of England.

Mentioned in the *Domesday* the Latin name for Shambles is *in Macello*. Along with nearby Whipmawhopmagate perhaps one of the most famous streets in the world and the most visited street in Europe. In 2010 it won the Google Britain's Most Picturesque Street Award. Shambles was originally called Haymongergate to signify the hay that was here to feed the livestock before slaughter; after that it was called Needlergate after the needles made here from the bones of slaughtered animals. It gets its present name (at first The Great Flesh Shambles) from the fleshammels – a shammel being the wooden board butchers used to display their meat on. They would throw their past-sell-by-date meat, offal, blood and guts into the runnel in the middle of the street to add to the mess caused by chamber pot disposal from the overhanging jetties. In 1280 seventeen butchers paid an annual shammel toll of seventy shillings between them; in 1872 25 out of the 39 shops here were butchers out of a total of 88 in the whole of York. There were also four pubs: The Globe (closed 1936); The Eagle and Child (closed 1925); The Neptune (closed 1903) and The Shoulder of Mutton (closed 1898). The street is narrow by design, to keep the sun off the meat.

PETER LANE YORK

Peter Lane is a typical York snickelway, in this photo looking out onto Ousegate. It is named after St. Peter-the-Little (Eccelsia S. Petri Parva). A lane led off from here to the 'Great Shambles', but it was 'stopped up' early in Elizabeth I's reign; on 29th January, 'the sixteenth of Elizabeth', it was divided 'into twelve parcels for tenements, adjoining it, the occupiers whereof, were to pay a small yearly rent for ever … and keep it clear of filth'. Peter Lane turns into Le Kyrk Lane, Pope's Head Alley, or Peter Lane Little (a nod to the church); at 80 cm wide, this is one of the narrowest and gloomiest ginnels in York, although it is illuminated by an old-fashioned-looking lantern. The church belonged to the Bishops of Durham in 1121-1228. Over time graves belonging to the church have been plundered: in 1884 bones were removed as souvenirs and coffin lids pilfered to be used as baking boards. A rockery at 9 High Petergate benefitted from some stolen carved stones.

Joseph Aloysius Hansom (1842-1900), the architect and inventor of the Patent Safety Cabriolet that bears his name, was born at 114 Micklegate (below) and christened in the Bar Convent Chapel. He suffered from severe depression and shot himself in his office on 27th May 1900. A pub in Market Street was named after him. Architecturally, Hansom's best known work is probably the majestic neoclassical Birmingham Town Hall. The Hansom Cab was so common a sight that Disraeli called it 'the gondola of London'.

A famous Hayes photo showing Mickelgate.

Pavement with All Saints in the background, notable for its fascinating lantern tower – a 15th century beacon guiding travellers in to the city from the outlying areas, notably the dark and dangerous Forest of Galtres. The north door sanctuary knocker shows a lion devouring a sinner.

The ancient Golden Fleece still survives (with its impressive golden sheep hanging above the door) on Pavement – as does the 15th century timber-framed Tudor mansion in the centre, once the home of Thomas Herbert, Bart. born there in 1606. To the right is Rowntree's shop; members of the family lived above. The pub is reputedly haunted, home to no fewer than seven ghosts. Earliest mention is in the City Archive of 1503; it originally belonged to The Merchant Adventurers' who named it to celebrate their thriving woollen trade. In 1702, John Peckett, Lord Mayor owned it. The building has incomplete foundations which accounts in part for its lop-sidedness.

On most Saturdays there were auction sales in Pavement: 'Not the least interesting was the sale of a woman [in 1839]. She had left her husband through his drunken habits and ill-treatment, and in one of his mad freaks he had brought her into the Market-place…with a halter round her neck. She was mounted on a table beside the auctioneer, who descanted on her virtues and spoke of her as a clean, industrious, quiet and careful woman, attractive in appearance and well mannered'. She went for 7s 6d, halter included, and proceeded to live with her purchaser near to Pavement. Twenty years later her husband died and she married said purchaser; she herself died in the 1880s 'at a great age, respectable and respected'.

Pavement is called thus because around 1329 it was the only clear piece of paved land in the centre of the city. Paving was unusual then. Before that it was called Marketshire and was the site of markets (there once was a market cross here). Proclamations and public punishments took place here in days when the punishment was made, and seen, to fit the crime: for example, drunks were made to stand on barrels with pint pots on their heads and goose thieves were put in the stocks with goose wings

draped unceremoniously around their necks. Catholic Thomas Percy, Earl of Northumberland, was executed here in 1572 for his opposition to Elizabeth I. Another fine York Market Cross in Pavement was consigned to the 19th century equivalent of a skip. The Market Cross was demolished in 1813 to make room for more market stalls. Isaac Poad was a potato merchant here. Today the family still runs a grain and seed business at Cattal near York with a contract brewery side producing a range of Isaac Poad beers and gins. One of the most heinous acts of Victorian civic vandalism to be visited on a city was the dynamiting of the cupola-topped St. Crux in Pavement in 1887 on health and safety grounds.

College Street. The priests in Bedern had been indulging in 'colourful nocturnal habits' and were re-billeted in the nearby college so that their behaviour could be monitored more closely. One incident involved one of the cathedral freelances hitting a man over the head with the blunt end of an axe. Charles I established his propaganda Royal printing house here during the Civil War and it was used as the Royal Mint at one time.

St. Sampson's Square or Brown's Corner was a slave market in late Roman times. Brown's was founded by Henry Rhodes Brown in 1891 and has been here since 1900. During the Civil War Cromwell's army 'shot well nigh forty Hot Fiery bullets' into the square, one of which 'slewe a maide'. The square was the venue for the Thursday hardware market and boasted a fine market cross until its demolition in the 1830s. Plays were staged here on the upper floor. The sign on The Three Cranes pub in the square is designed to mislead: the pub is named after the lifting gear used by stallholders rather than anything ornithological. The Roman Bath was formerly The Mail Coach, The Barrel Churn, The Cooper and The Barrel. The Roman bathhouse excavated here in 1930 is partly visible, including cold room: *frigidarium*, hot room: *caldarium* and underfloor central heating system: *hypocaust*. Tiles stamped Legio VI and Legio IX have been uncovered recording which legions were stationed at Eboracum. There is a small but superb museum under the pub.

At the junction of King's Court and Newgate, Pump Court was the site of one of the many water pumps and wells that served the city. Piped water was turned on in parts of the city between 1677 and 1685; a public bathhouse opened in 1691. John Wesley preached in a room (the 'Oven') here in 1753 (one of 26 visits to the city); it became an official place of worship for Methodists in 1754. One of the country's only two surviving lantern tower windows is in Pump Court, tragically, almost hidden from public view. Betty Petre lived here; she kept her cattle in the court before slaughter in Shambles; Mr. Huber collected sheeps' guts and washed them in a drain before exporting them to Germany to make fiddle strings. Other residents included a chimney sweep and a prostitute, referred to locally as 'an old knock'.

The Unitarian Chapel was built in 1693 in St. Saviourgate four years after the Act of Toleration legalised non-conformist places of worship. Originally built for Presbyterians by Lady Sarah Hewley it is, unusually, in the shape of a Greek cross.

King's Staith in 1966 with the Ship (opened 1787, now long closed) and the Kings Arms in view. Over the years there have been fourteen pubs in York named the Ship, and four Slips. Not bad for a land-locked city; it reflects the commercial importance of the rivers here and, in the case of Strensall, the navigation. The Kings Arms is an early 17th century building on King's Staith, traditionally a hotbed of crime and prostitution. Originally, the pub had no fireplaces or room partitions so it may have been a custom house, or a warehouse. Very thick walls protect it from floods, which recur with alarming regularity. Due to the flooding, the cellars are on the first floor. Bodies of criminals were laid out here before being hung on and then flung from old Ouse Bridge just along the staith. It was first recorded as a pub in 1783 or 1795 as the Kings Arms; then in the 19th century licensee George Duckitt renamed it as Ouse Bridge Inn. It reverted to its old name in 1974. The inn sign depicts King Richard III, who as a boy grew up at Middleham Castle, and as Duke of Gloucester visited York frequently from his castle at Sheriff

Hutton. He was very popular in York. The Kings Arms is famously 'the pub that floods'; it is the pub that is never dry. On the right hand side of the door is a board with the flood levels marked on it. In 2000 the water was six feet deep in the bar, deep enough to drown your sorrows in. Every time York floods – and that's a lot of times – the pub provides the backdrop for news reports the world over.

Davygate 1929. A vintage car to die for outside the famous Davy Hall Restaurant built in 1904 by George Edward Barton and designed by architects Penty and Penty who described it as being in a "distinct art nouveau style with a much talked about stained glass canopy". Davygate is named after David le Lardiner (clerk of the kitchen). His job was to stock the King's larder; in the 12th century David's father, John, was the Royal lardiner for the Forest of Galtres – a title which became hereditary – David  received land from King Stephen in 1135. Davygate was also the site of the forest courthouse prison – the only one in the land for incarcerating transgressors of Forest of Galtres laws. It was on Davygate in Davy Hall. The Wheatsheaf in Davygate was at one time the residence of the Bishops of Durham.

Originally Joubrettagate – the Street of the Bretons in the Jewish Quarter – and Jubretgate. Over the years occupants have included Webster's kitchen and bath-ware shop which became Pawson's, specialists in rubber-ware; The White Rose Inn which became Forrington's furnishers around 1920. At one stage in its life it was home to six families. Jubbergate originally extended to cover what is today Market Street as far as Coney Street. York's first police station was here until 1880 when it moved to Clifford Street.

For many years Walmgate was a place of great poverty, crime, alcohol-related violence and prostitution, like Hungate. The infant mortality rate was one in three before age one – as highlighted by Seebohm Rowntree's ground-breaking *Poverty: A Study in Town Life* in 1901 for which researchers visited 11,500 families and found that 25% of the city population was visibly poor – in 'obvious want and squalor'. The pungent smell of hide, skins and fat from local industries added to the horror of the place. At the end of the 1880s there were 8,000 midden privies in York, many here and in Hungate. In Walmgate in 1913, the death rate was 23 per 1,000, almost twice York's average. Using powers under the 1930 Housing Act, York Corporation began to clear the slums: streets off Walmgate and in Hungate were demolished, and residents moved to new estates outside the city centre.

Queen's Staith 1973. What looks like a shanty town actually illustrates how important the River Ouse is to tourism and commerce in the city.

Museum Street. Traffic was always a problem – just a different kind in the 60s. © *York Press*.

The west front of the Minster (below), partially hidden by the buildings in Lop Lane – which were demolished to create Duncombe Place. The Dispensary was built between 1860 and 1864 by demolishing buildings on the corner of Blake Street and Lop Lane, or Flea Alley. Duncombe Place was named after Dean Augustus Duncombe in 1858; he himself subscribed £1,000 to help finance the building of the Place. St. Wilfrid's Church was completed in 1864. The York Dispensary, set up to look after York's sick poor (the County Hospital had no remit there), was originally in the Merchant Adventurers' Hall, moving to St. Andrewgate and then, in 1828, to New Street. The next move was to the majestic, often overlooked, red brick building in Duncombe Place in 1851. Its noble mission, as recorded in *Baines' Directory* for 1823, was 'to dispense gratuitously advice, medicine and surgical assistance, to those who are unable to pay for them'. Medicines were free of charge and 600 or so children were vaccinated here 'without cost for the smallpox'. The corporation contributed £5 towards an apothecary's shop and one guinea a year for five years. After 30 or so years 42,488 patients had been seen with 28,851 cured.

Napoleon arrived in York in 1822, one year after his death on St. Helena, to stand sentinel outside a tobacconists in Low Ousegate, H. Clarke, to whom letters were addressed simply as 'Napoleon, York' – and would arrive. In full uniform, he is proffering a snuff box to passers-by. Bonaparte was carved out of a solid piece of oak and was one of three made, selling for £50 each. Apparently he frequently ended up in the River Ouse, courtesy of soldiers garrisoned in York.

— LADY PECKETT'S PASSAGE —

Lady Peckett's Yard connects Fossgate with Pavement and is named after the wife of John Peckett, a Lord Mayor of York. It was called Bacusgail (Bake House Lane) in 1312 and later housed an auctioneers and Richardson's, a money lender. In 1857 Joseph Rowntree II rented a building in the yard for one of his many adult schools where men were taught to read and write, using scripture lessons; women were admitted soon after. Mary Kitching was president of the 'B' class of Lady Peckett's Yard Ladies School for fourteen years until in 1892 she left to do missionary work in the Holy Land. A lion from a circus in Parliament Street escaped and was eventually cornered here in the early 1900s. Nearby in Black Horse Passage Joseph Rowntree set up a soup kitchen in 1845. The Bluebell, York's smallest pub, is in Fossgate. It was built in 1798 when the back of the pub faced on to Fossgate and the front was in Lady Peckett's Yard. The Rowntrees were responsible for turning it around in 1903, no doubt because one of their Adult schools was in Lady Peckett's Yard. York City FC held their board meetings here; in the Second World War it served as a soup kitchen. Women were refused admission to the public bar until the 1990s.

The Assembly Rooms, Blake Street, can be seen on the left in this 1906 photograph. One of the earliest neo-classical buildings in Europe in Blake Street, the 1732 Assembly Rooms were designed by the Earl of Burlington in the Palladian style and were paid for by subscription to provide the local gentry with somewhere sumptuous to play dice and cards, dance and drink tea, as featured in Smollett's *The Expedition of Humphrey Clinker*. The building epitomised the age of elegance and helped make York the capital of north country fashion – a northern Bath. The main hall is surrounded by 48 magnificent Corinthian pillars. Sedan chair men met in the cellars here; it was requisitioned by the Food Office in 1939. In 1751 the seats from the aisles were removed to the front of the columns for use by ladies with wide hooped skirts, too wide for them to pass between the columns, as pointed out by the Duchess of Marlborough. This was much to the disgust of Hermit in York who, in 1823, described them as fit only for 'the market women of Covent Garden'.

Sorting the mail in York's sorting office in the early 70s.

Craven's originated in 1803 when Joseph Hick set up as a 29 year old in York as Kilner and Hick, confectioners. Kilner left town leaving Hick with the business which he relocated to 47 Coney Street next door to what was then the Leopard Inn, opposite St Martin le Grand. Mary Ann Hick was born in 1829 and in 1851 she married Thomas Craven who had served an apprenticeship with George Berry, later a partner at Terry's; he bought a building in Pavement from William Dove and a further site at 10 Coppergate, both of which expanded his own confectionery business. In 1860 Joseph Hick died and his estate was divided up between his three children. In 1862 Mary Ann's husband died leaving her with three young children to raise and two businesses to run. Near to starvation she took up the challenge, amalgamated the businesses, changed the name of the company to MA Craven, and ran it until her death in 1902. In 1881 her son, Joseph William, joined the firm which became MA Craven & Son. There were four Craven's retail shops in the city, one of which, Craven's Mary Ann Sweet Shop, was in the Shambles and featured a sweet museum on the first floor where visitors could see 150 years of the 'Art, Trade, Mystery and Business of the Confectioner'. Today the Craven brand is owned by Tangerine Confectionery which manufacturers sugar confectionery from their plant in Low Poppleton Lane.

A cattle market has existed here from the 15th century. The opening in 1855 of the six acre cattle market in Paragon Street led to the reopening of Fishergate Bar to enable cattle to be driven through; it also saw the end of the time-honoured practice of keeping livestock behind butchers' shops and slaughtered on site, as happened in Shambles for many years. The market building comprised 44 pens which could hold 616 fat cattle, some less fat ones and 6,750 sheep. It served the city for nearly 150 years when it moved to Murton after closing in 1971; it was demolished in 1976. The Barbican Centre, refurbished in 2011, was built on part of the cattle market site in the late 1970s.

The Poor Clares. The cameraman looks as though he is inflicting some kind of torture on these poor nuns. The first convent of the Sisters of the Second Order of Saint Francis was in Hull Road in 1865; they moved to the obscure St. Joseph's Convent in Lawrence Street in 1875 where, until recently, they lived behind twenty-feet high walls, got up at 5.00am, lived for the most part in silence, went to bed at 8.00pm, ventured outside only when absolutely necessary, were vegetarians and cultivated a six-acre garden. The buildings were designed by a local Roman Catholic ecclesiastical artist, George Goldie, between 1870 and 1875. In December 1985 the then Mother Abbess, Sister Mary Bernard, spoke to *Evening Press* reporter Simon Schofield about daily life in the convent – and preparations for Christmas. Speaking through the iron bars that separated the convent from the outside world, she described the Christmas presents the nuns would receive. "The presents would probably horrify most people," she said. "We might get a packet of soap powder, or some bars of soap, or some toothpaste – things we need." © *York Press*.

One marvellous production which rolled out of York Carriage Works was the ambulance train made from existing carriage rolling stock; it comprised sixteen carriages and was known as 'Continental Ambulance Train Number 37'. It was 890 feet 8 inches long and weighed 465 tons when loaded, without a locomotive. Painted khaki it bore the Geneva Red Cross painted on the window panels and frames on each of the carriages on both sides. It features as a wonderful exhibit in the museum. Overall, the ambulance car could carry between 445 and 659 patients and staff, depending on how it was configured. Obviously, good ventilation, light and infection control were paramount; there

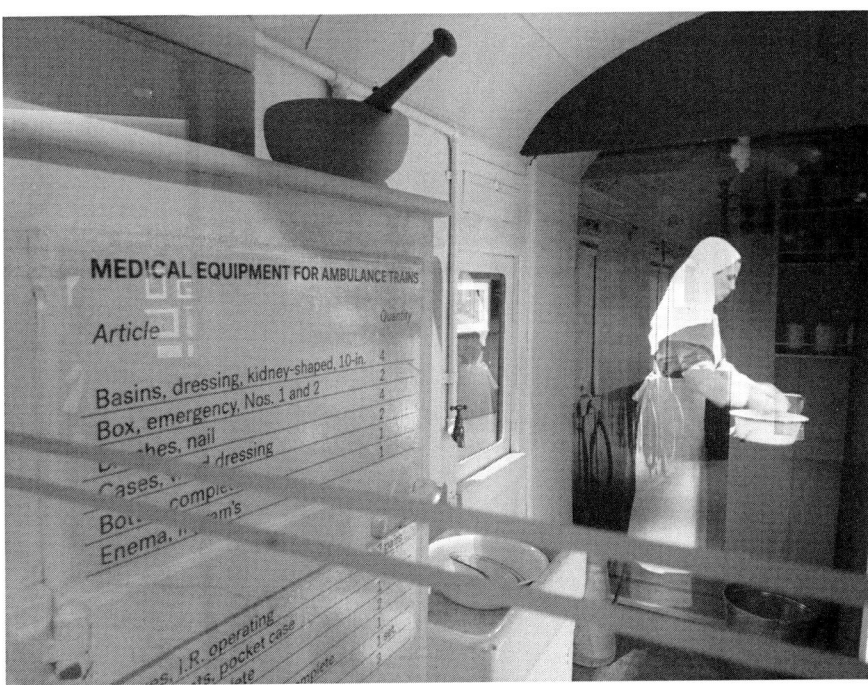

were electric fans everywhere with extra ones for gassed patients. To promote hygiene, round corners were used and the toilets, wash rooms and treatment room all had concrete floors. The kitchen was floored with lead while other areas were covered in linoleum. A smooth ride was essential for the injured: to that end the train had bolster, side bearing and auxiliary springs on the four wheeled bogies which ran on 'patent cushioned wheels'.

Gas lighting, or 'the lamp that wouldn't blow out', was introduced to York by the York Gas Light Company in 1824 on the banks of the River Foss near Monk Bridge. In 1836 the York Union Gas Light Company was formed; rivalry was intense with workmen from the former going round digging up or filling in the latter's excavations; the two companies eventually amalgamated in 1837 to form the York United Gas Light Company in Hungate. In 1824 there were 250 consumers; this had risen to 34,000 by 1963. By 1841 the two companies had amalgamated as the York Union Gaslight Company, at Fossbank and in 1883 they moved to offices in Davygate. In 1912 coverage was extended to seven miles from the Ouse Bridge to take in Haxby, Wigginton and Strensall.

The earliest railway building at York was the York and North Midland Company two-road engine shed built in 1839; it soon was integrated into one of the Queen Street workshops. The York and North Midland Company built the locomotive repair shop in Queen Street in 1842; small carriage repair and carriage painting shops were also built in Queen Street in 1849 – this was all closed in 1905 when NER focused locomotive construction in Darlington. Older locomotives were upgraded at Queen Street; the works also carried out construction and repair of carriages and wagons and by 1864 was turning out 100 wagons per week. To cope with demand, wagon shops between Holgate and Leeman Roads opened on a seventeen acre site in 1865 to build engines and tenders, extended in 1875. In 1876 output stood at 102 carriages, 2,387 wagons, 419 engines built with 2,865 carriages and 22,185 wagons repaired. Weekly pay bill was £2,500 between a workforce of 1,600. Larger premises were built in 1884 around Holgate Road when it was decided to concentrate more carriage building at York; these were its busiest times and by 1910 the works covered 45 acres.

Clearing the terraces. York City FC was formed in 1922, and played in the Midland League for seven years before joining the Football League. They played their first two home matches at Mille Crux, Haxby Road, before moving into Fulfordgate on Heslington Lane from 1922, in 1932 leasing land at Bootham Crescent from York Cricket Club as a replacement for their ground at Fulfordgate. Bootham Crescent has a capacity of 8,256. In the Second World War, the Popular Stand was converted into an air-raid shelter, and the ground suffered slight damage when a bomb landed on houses along the Shipton Street End. © *York Press.*

Bettys. The story of Bettys begins in September 1907 when a twenty-two year old Fritz Butzer arrived in England from Switzerland with no English and less of any idea of how to reach a town that sounded vaguely like 'Bratwurst', where a job awaited him. Fritz eventually landed up in Bradford and found work with a Swiss confectioners called Bonnet & Sons at 44 Darley Street. Cashing in on the vogue for all things French, Fritz changed his name to Frederick Belmont; he opened his first business in July 1919 – a cafe in Cambridge Crescent, Harrogate, on three floors fitted out to the highest standards. In 1936 Frederick travelled on the maiden voyage of *The Queen Mary*. He was so impressed that he commissioned the ship's designers to turn what had been an old furniture shop in York into his

most sophisticated tea rooms – and that is what you still get in the art deco upstairs function room. The neo-Georgian building in St. Helen's Square was fitted out by Ward and Leckenby in 1937. JE Mcdonald was the first of many airmen to scratch their names on the mirror here in what became known as the Briefing Room during the Second World War, in February 1945. © *York Press*.

Cooke, Troughton & Simms – Optical Instrument Manufacturers. In 1856 Cooke moved into the Buckingham Works built on the site of the home of the second Duke of Buckingham at Bishophill – one of Britain's first purpose-built telescope factories. He built a telescope for Prince Albert in 1860 and one for a Gateshead millionaire: the telescope tube was 32 feet long and the whole instrument weighed nine tons: the biggest telescope in the world at the time. In 1893 H.D. Taylor, Optical Manager, designed the Cooke Photographic Lens which became the basic design for most camera lenses thereafter. In 1866 Thomas Cooke branched out into three-wheeled steam cars which reached the dizzy speed of fifteen mph; they, were, however, outlawed by the Road Act which prohibited vehicles which travelling in excess of four mph. In those days a man with a red flag had to walk in front of any vehicle not pulled by a horse. Cooke fitted his steam engine into a boat and travelled on the Ouse, free of horses and red flags. He died in 1868.

Leetham's Mill Warehouse at Hungate was one of the largest flour mills in Europe and was designed by Walter Penty in 1895 comprising five storeys and a nine storey water tower complete with battlements and turrets. It is surrounded on three sides by the Foss and Wormald's Cut. By 1911 more than 600 people worked here. Spillers took it over in 1930 before removing to Hull in 1931 after a fire; Rowntrees bought it in 1937 for cocoa bean storage.

JB Richardson, Harnessmaker in 1913. This wonderful shop on the corner of Monkgate and Lord Mayor's Walk later became Bulmer's, another wonderful shop. Now it is apartments.